SOURCE DOCUMENTS IN AMERICAN LUTHERAN HYMNODY

SOURCE DOCUMENTS IN AMERICAN LUTHERAN HYMNODY

Carl F. Schalk

CPH
SAINT LOUIS

Library of Congress Cataloging-in-Publication Data

Source documents in American Lutheran hymnody / [edited, annotated,
    and translated by] Carl F. Schalk.
            p.   cm.
    Includes bibliographical references.
    ISBN 0-570-01352-6
        1. Lutheran Church—United States—Hymns—History and criticism—
Sources.   2. Hymns, English—United States—History and criticism—
Sources.   3. Hymns, German—United States—History and criticism—
Sources.   4. Hymns, Scandinavian—United States—History and
criticism— Sources.   I. Schalk, Carl.
BV410.S68   1996
264′ . 0417302—dc20   95-10541

1 2 3 4 5 6 7 8 9 10   05 04 03 02 01 00 99 98 97 96

For my students,
past and present,
who have explored with me the fascination
of Lutheran hymnody in America

Contents

Movements Toward a More Confessional Hymnody

Movements Toward Consensus and Consolidation

Introduction

This collection of source documents in American Lutheran hymnody is an attempt to bring together for the first time in one place the prefaces and introductions to the most significant Lutheran hymnals and choralebooks that have been produced in America, from Muhlenberg's *Erbauliche Liedersammlung* (1786) to *Christian Worship: A Lutheran Hymnal* (1993). In most instances these prefaces shed a good deal of light on the hymnic situation of the church at the time and frequently provide rich insight into the contemporary movements and motivations that prompted each subsequent book. While this book is intended as a companion volume to *God's Song in a New Land: Lutheran Hymnals in America*, it certainly may be read profitably on its own.

The documents presented here are taken, for the most part, from the official books of the various Lutheran church bodies. Inclusion of material from the countless occasional hymnals, Sunday School hymnbooks, and similar sources would have expanded the size of this collection beyond reasonable bounds. These other areas, while not included in this collection, offer a rich field for the study of their impact on hymnic traditions of America's Lutherans.

German, English, and Norwegian materials are included. The translations—with the exception of the three documents translated from the Norwegian by Gerhard Cartford—are the work of the editor. While the German and Norwegian prefaces have been translated into English, the titles in the original languages have been retained together with their translation at the beginning of those selections. While the editor remains responsible for the translations and notes, special thanks must be acknowledged to the following: to Daniel Poellot (+) and F. Samuel Janzow who offered comments on several of the translations; to Hilton Oswald who carefully checked the German translations for accuracy and offered valuable suggestions for making them more readable; and to Gerhard Cartford who graciously allowed use of his translations of the three Norwegian documents.

The various selections are grouped around four major developments in American Lutheran hymnody: the transplanting of Lutheran hymnody to America; the accommodation to the American scene and the movements of rationalism, unionism, and revivalism in the early years of the 19th century; the Confessional revival in the later years of the 19th century; and the movement toward consolidation and unification that began in the later 19th century and that has continued to the present. While some duplication of material found in these sources documents and in the texts of *God's Song in a New Land* will be inevitable, it is hoped that it will not prove to be redundant.

Annotations giving additional background information or placing some of the events described more clearly in the light of their time may be of particular interest to students of American Lutheran hymnody. To an extent the selection of materials in a collection such as this is always somewhat arbitrary. It is hoped, however, that these selections will be of assistance in grasping more clearly the various currents that have helped to shape the course of Lutheran hymnody in America in the past two hundred years.

Carl Schalk

1

Erbauliche Liedersammlung[1]

Henry Melchior Muhlenberg's Erbauliche Liedersammlung *of 1786 was the first Lutheran hymnal to be published in America specifically for use by Lutherans in the new land. Muhlenberg, often referred to as the "father of American Lutheranism," organized the Pennsylvania Ministerium in 1748 and was the chief shaper of its first hymn book and wrote its Preface.*

Erbauliche Liedersammlung

zum Gottesdienstlichen Gebrauch in den Vereinigten Evangelisch Lutherischen Gemeinen in Pennsylvanien und den benachbarten Staaten

Gesammelt, eingerichtet, und zum Druck befördert durch die gesamten Glieder des hiesigen Vereinigten Evangelisch-Lutherischen Ministeriums, 1786.

A Collection of Devotional Hymns

For Use in the Worship of the United Evangelical Lutheran Congregations in Pennsylvania and Neighboring States

Collected, arranged, and prepared for publication by the local German Evangelical Lutheran Ministerium, 1786.

Dear Christian Reader,

The honorable Evangelical Ministerium in Pennsylvania has enjoined me to write a preface for this collection of hymns.[2] But what new thing can I, a tired and worn old man of 75 years,[3] say that has not already been said with more thoroughness, taste, and edification, and that has not been made to serve the common good in countless prefaces?

I should be pleased if I could now make some comments regarding the correct use of this spiritual treasury of psalms and hymns. However, space and my incapacity will permit only a few remarks.

1. Talented and gifted teachers will choose for public worship such hymns as are suited for mixed assemblies and, so far as possible, agree with the truths they are intended to support, clarifying them and making them impressive.

2. It is eminently to be desired that all singers, both men and women, in public and private worship, remain conscious of the meaning of the text, and that when they proclaim the words with their mouth and lips, they also think about them and be sensitive to their meaning; otherwise this passage quoted in Matt. 15:8 applies: "This people draweth near to Me with their mouth and honoreth Me with their lips, but their heart is far from Me." Also Amos 5:23.

3. Experienced and faithful pastors also do well to take the opportunity to explain the core-hymns (*Kernlieder*), to develop their concepts, and to seek to make the hymns comprehensible to the souls entrusted to their care; to do so will not remain without profit and blessing. Whoever does not do this may be compared to a man who gives hard nuts to little children or old people—who have no teeth—in order to satisfy their hunger. One notices quite quickly if the mouth alone sings without the devotion of the heart, when, for example, a bird flies through the assembly or someone happens to come in during the singing, then the mouth indeed continues to sing thoughtlessly, but the eyes and thoughts are immediately fixed on the slightest foreign object. Souls hungry and thirsty for mercy are not so easily led astray.

4. It is to be hoped that the singing may be conducted in a chaste and harmonious manner in all public assemblies, as it is in some. Many still have the custom of straining every muscle and singing everything with might and main, which could more appropriately be called a braying or roaring, as Elijah said to the servants of Baal, I Kings 19:27[4]: "Cry louder. Perhaps your idol is sleeping." Through such forced singing one drowns out one's own thoughts, disturbs the congregation in its devotion, tires out one's body, and causes negative sensations in one's neighbor. Moses, the man of God, made no great yelling when he was in distress; rather he uttered his heart's concern before Jehovah with a sighing voice, and the Lord had such a delicate and penetrating ear that he answered Moses: "Wherefore criest thou unto me?" 2 Moses 14:15.[5] "He that planted the ear, shall He not hear?" Ps. 94.[6] The pattern most worthy of imitation is given by St. Paul, Eph. 5: "Be filled with the Spirit, namely with His gifts and influences, speaking in your assemblies and in private in psalms and hymns and spiritual songs, singing and playing to the Lord in your hearts."[7] Thus the right use of the spiritual is joined together with the poetic and musical arts. The most gracious Creator planted in most of the children of men a capacity and tendency to sing in four voices, named bass, tenor, alto, and discant by the musicians. When such talents are cultivated, refined, and sanctified in Christian schools, they later serve for revival, encouragement, and edification in Christian congregations, and they produce sweet harmony and a foretaste of heavenly pleasures in all who recognize and love the spiritual in music or who have a musical ear.

5. We should note what until now has hindered complete unity in connection with singing in our public worship, namely, the many kinds of hymnbooks,[8] since in almost every one various little alterations have been made, and in some there are few hymns, in others many. If only there were one hymnbook for all American congregations that would contain the best of the old and new spiritual songs, how much more convenient and harmonious it would be. And why should the evangelical congregations not have the authority and right to introduce their own hymnbook, as long as they still enjoy the priceless freedom of religion and conscience? What matters is not the number of hymns, but rather the choice of the best and most powerful, and

for that we still have—thank God—freedom and opportunity, as sensible and experienced Christians can themselves perceive from this book.

6. With regard to the art of poetry and music, there will always be something to cultivate and improve so that its highest stage of perfection will seem to be reserved for that time when the earth will be full of a lively knowledge of Jesus Christ, and people will be singing in the highest choir: "Lord, our Lord, how excellent is Thy name in all the earth, etc."[9] "Now shall the salvation and the strength and the riches and the power of our God become those of Christ."[10] Dan. 2:44, 45. Micah 4:1, 2, 7.[11]

7. In the meantime, beloved souls, sing and play to the Lord, who has purchased you with His blood; sing and pray in your hearts, publicly and individually; believe and live with all other remaining true Christians in all parts of the world, running the race until you reach the heavenly choir in the land of the blessed. That which is truly godly in this treasury of hymns shows us the way that has been prepared and the means for the journey to eternal life, how on this road we may enter the narrow gate, continuing on this road by God's power through suffering and conflict, and, finishing our course, may remain faithful unto death, enabled as conquerors to inherit the crown. Share this treasury of hymns with your children and your children's children that they may not come forward on the great day of judgment and complain against you and say, "You provided us with nourishment for our bodies, and with clothes, but our souls you forgot and neglected. Woe to us and you."

8. Besides, there is hardly an old or new core-hymn in existence in the Christian church that has not already been of service and blessing to man's soul. Psalms, hymns, and spiritual songs have demonstrated their godly power with the first Christians under the most cruel persecutions and most painful martyrdom, in imprisonment, at the stake, in all kinds of violent death because of their steadfast confession of the true Christian religion. Especially in the Reformation by the sainted Luther and his faithful co-workers has the Holy Spirit shown Himself mightily fruitful through psalms and spiritual songs. These are now called the old hymns. They were then very well suited to the circumstances of the time and very edifying. And they are still

so today, provided one still has a sound taste for the genuine truths of the faith and salvation. The newer hymns are more polished, according as the Christian moral teaching, the German language, and the poetic art were from time to time widened, refined, and improved.

There is not enough space to give examples of the effect and blessing which each old or new hymn had for souls; this belongs among other things to a close and edifying association with awakened and pardoned Christians; more eminently, however, it belongs to those joyful remembrances and praises of God of the perfected saints before the throne of God in the kingdom of glory.

9. Finally, and at the close of my weary forty-four years of wandering and pilgrimage in this western land,[12] my heartfelt wish goes out humbly and beseechingly before the throne of grace.

New Providence,[13] 1786
D. Heinrich Melchior Muhlenberg
Senior of the Ministerium

Notes

[1]The first Lutheran hymnbook to be prepared and printed for use by German-speakIng Lutherans in America. It contained 706 hymns.

[2]The action of the 35th Convention of the Evangelical Lutheran Ministerium in North America meeting in Lancaster, Pennsylvania, on June 4, 1782, unanimously resolved "to have a new Hymn Book printed for our United Congregations." A committee of Revs. Muhlenberg. Sen., Kunze, Helmuth, and Muhlenberg. Jr., was appointed to carry out the work. Among the rules by which the committee was to consider itself "strictly bound" were the following:

1. As far as possible to follow the arrangement of the Halle Hymn Book.

2. Not to omit any of the old standard hymns, especially of Luther and Paul Gerhardt.

It was also resolved that "Senior Muhlenberg prepare the Preface, and that it be signed by all the United Preachers." The last part of this directive was obviously not carried out. See A. Spaeth, H. E. Jacobs, and G. F. Spicker (eds.), *Documentary History of the Evangelical Lutheran Ministerium of Pennsylvania and Adjacent States.* Proceedings of the Annual Convention from 1748 to 1821. Compiled and Translated from Records in the Archives and from the Written Protocols (Philadelphia: Board of Publication of the General Council of the

Evangelical Lutheran Church in North America, 1898), pp. 183 ff.

3Heinrich Melchior Muhlenberg (1711–87) was born and educated in Germany. He came to Philadelphia in 1742 to strengthen New World Lutheranism. In 1748 he founded the first Lutheran Synod in America, the Pennsylvania Ministerium. He is often called the "Patriarch of American Lutheranism."

4The reference is in error. It should be 1 Kings 18:27.

5Exodus 14:15.

6Psalm 94:9.

7Ephesians 5:18–19.

8Among the various German hymnbooks which the immigrants brought with them from their homeland, and with which Muhlenberg was confronted from the very beginning, were the Marburg hymnal (which, in various European editions was widely used throughout the colonies and was also printed in an American edition by Christopher Sauer in Germantown), the so-called "Coethen Songs," the Wuerttemberg hymnal of 1741, and the most widely known and used "Halle hymnal" of J. A. Freylinghausen in its several editions (1704, 1714, and 1741).

9Psalm 8:1

10Revelation 12:10.

11These additional passages refer to the establishment of the Lord's universal reign in the last days.

12Muhlenberg came to Philadelphia in 1742.

13New Providence (Trappe), New Hanover (Falkner's Swamp), and the congregation at Philadelphia had been united into one parish by John Christian Schulz. Muhlenberg spent his last years at New Providence and is buried next to the old Trappe church, which is still in existence.

2

Choral-Buch für die Erbauliche Liedersammlung

der Deutschen Evangelisch-Lutherischen Gemeinen in Nord-Amerika

Auf Ansuchen des Deutschen Evangelisch-Lutherischen Ministeriums, herausgegeben von der Corporation der St. Michaelis- und Zions- Gemeine, in Philadelphia

Philadelphia: Gedruckt bei Conrad Zentler und Georg Blake, 1813.

Chorale Book for a Collection of Devotional Hymns

of the German Evangelical Lutheran Congregations in North America

Published in Philadelphia by the Corporation of St. Michael's and Zion Congregation at the request of the German Evangelical Lutheran Ministerium

Philadelphia: Conrad Zentler and Georg Blake, 1813.

Preface

Whoever considers, even superficially, the situation of the German Evangelical Church in this western country sees with astonishment how the Lord has most graciously visited His church with His blessing. One church after the other is being built, and one congregation after another is being founded; not a year goes by in which developments of this nature are not manifested.

Nor does the Lord permit a lack of those who, each in his own way, dedicate themselves to His service. He stirs up young men who preach the Gospel with clear perception and lead the manifold flocks of the Lord Jesus to the pasture of God's Word.

There appeared to be only one great deficiency common to all our congregations: the singing, the most powerful means of edification in our congregations, was indeed inadequate. Some congregations had one form of the melodies, others had another. One would hear almost as many different melodies in our services as there were congregations; in one place people sang too fast, in another too slowly.

For some years our Ministerium had thought about the preparation of a chorale-melody book arranged specifically for our hymnbook. However, men were always lacking with sufficient skills, spirit, and willingness for such an undertaking until a committee of the German Evangelical Lutheran Congregation in Philadelphia took the work in hand and, with the assistance of a venerable and very skillful musician under the supervision of the corporation of the above-mentioned congregation, undertook the project and brought it to a happy conclusion.[1] How blessed the results of this two-year work in our congregation has been can be perceived by anyone who compares our singing now with before. The book is now ready and one could hardly find a better book of its kind.

May the Lord in His grace bless this undertaking and arouse all God-fearing men who have influence in their congregations that they be concerned that with the assistance of this work the singing prevailing in our congregations may be found ever more lovely and uniform for the common edification.

Upon order of St. Michael and Zion Corporation
of Philadelphia
J. Heinr. Ch. Helmuth, President

Introduction

The Reason for the Publication of This Chorale Book

Since the publication of our Lutheran hymnbook,[2] people had the unpleasant experience that, because of a lack of a chorale book, chorale melodies introduced in our churches several centuries ago are sung one way in one church and another way in other churches. Furthermore, since people saw that many old, powerful melodies were entirely forgotten here and there, and since there were no melodies at hand at all for a large number of the hymns and therefore these could never be sung in public worship, it was thought that through the publication of this chorale book these circumstances unfavorable to congregational singing might be alleviated.

Who Has Undertaken This Publication and Why?

In order to achieve this ultimate purpose, a committee of musically knowledgeable men was formed more than four years ago in Philadelphia. This committee endeavored to choose and assemble appropriate, pleasing, and simple melodies for our hymnbook, with the purpose that this collection might perhaps in the future be made generally useful through its publication, if the time and circumstances for such an undertaking would appear to be propitious. In order to guarantee results in the work, these melodies were always practiced beforehand with the choir* established here, and then first were they introduced to the congregation, which now sings most of the melodies, not only correctly and acceptably, but also with delight and edification.

*A choir, even one that is able to sing only the melody and is composed of mostly women's voices, is an absolute necessity for the introduction of new melodies, as it is for the overall improvement of congregational singing. New melodies should be practiced beforehand by the choir, and when learned they should be sung a number of times in a moderate voice and with a moderate tempo, either at the beginning or the close of worship. The congregation merely listens and only later is encouraged to alternate with the choir in the singing of the new melody. Old melodies, which in most congregations have largely been sung in a dragging fashion and with altogether too many interpolations, are likewise taught to the congregation according to the directions of the chorale book by following the aforementioned procedure. The congregation is made mindful of this beforehand and then invited to sing along voluntarily. In the country, where the congregation always assembles quite a while before the service begins, it would certainly be profitable if old and young would always unite with the organist or precentor and sing through one or the other melody with feeling and grace.

The Number of Melodies
and Their Composers

The number of these melodies runs to approximately 270,[3] and these consist in part of old melodies from Koenig's chorale book[4] and others; in part of new melodies taken from Gregor's, Knecht's, and Vierling's choral books;[5] and in part also of entirely new compositions that were necessary because the old melodies that were at hand either appeared too difficult to introduce or were not appropriate for the song, or because many a completely new meter had no melody available at all.

The Arrangement of This Chorale Book
According to Meter

Concerning the arrangement of this chorale book, it is necessary to note that the melodies found in this book are arranged according to meter, so that all melodies that belong to one meter have the same syllable pattern for each stanza and thus may be substituted one for another. An example will illustrate this best. Open the book to pages 1–4, meter two. Here are seven melodies that have one and the same rhythm or meter, and in the appendix there appears still another that likewise belongs here, making eight. These eight melodies are called fundamental melodies because all other hymns that belong to this meter can be sung to one or the other of these fundamental melodies. The index shows which fundamental melody may be most suitable for this or that hymn, however, without attempting to bind the hands of the craftsman in the free use of the melodies, since he instinctively knows that, for example, the melody "Salvation Unto Us Has Come" is not appropriate to the penitential hymn "Lord Jesus Christ, Thou Highest Good."

Concerning the Meters
and Their Associated Melodies in Particular

Anyone who carefully examines the second meter just referred to and the eight melodies it contains will find that the number of melodies is not too large. In part this is because all of these melodies have been sung in our church for a long time and had to be retained so that they may not fall completely into oblivion, partly because these are beautiful, powerful melodies, and finally because our hymnbook contains 64 hymns that can be sung to this meter. Accordingly a large number of hymns necessitates a proportionately large number of melodies, so much the more because the content of the hymns is different. Therefore this relation must also be found with reference to the melodies and their character. In short, there must be melodies available that suit the number and content of the hymns at hand. This observation holds true equally in reference to all meters. It remains to be noted that many meters have an additional beautiful new melody, and that for this reason two melodies are occasionally furnished, an old one and a new one. Whoever regards this as superfluous, or is fascinated only with the old and will hear nothing that is new, should please consider that with the publishing of this chorale book consideration was at the same time given to the singing schools,[6] which should find in this collection a rich supply of beautiful new melodies which they may conveniently sing in church in two, three, and four parts.

Concerning the Appendix

The appendix would not really have been necessary. But then, a beautiful new melody was found here and there and one wanted to give it wider circulation. The meter of each of these is shown with the melody as well as in the index.

Remarks Concerning Fine Chorale Singing, Chiefly in Public Worship

In order to make this chorale book as complete as possible and to make it the more useful for everyone who will use this book as a vehicle to learn or to help improve congregational singing, the editors have considered it appropriate to include in this introduction a number of instructive hints concerning the nature of fine hymn singing and the means to make such beautiful song more universal. It is by no means their purpose to discuss this subject in detail: for that purpose the limits of a preface, if it were not considerably expanded, would be far too confining. But they wish merely to make only a few comments which are occasioned chiefly by the many mistakes that have been made in congregational singing throughout this country

Singing in the church, or at other occasions of worship, has as its purposes to elicit or promote devotion and to promote in the soul a solemn mood, so that it may be more receptive for celestial impressions and heavenly perceptions. It naturally follows that such a song must itself be devotional and solemn, that is, it must be executed slowly and with moderate voices, never with frivolous haste and unpleasant noise. Where the singing is an expression of the feelings of a faithful heart set toward God, it is not necessary first to lay down rules. But also people who do not have this attitude of the heart while they are present in religious assemblies should at least not dishonor a Christian gathering through improper song. When we sing spiritual songs, it is proper to sing them as if we were in God's presence. And who would not consider it the greatest impropriety in the presence of the Eternal and Almighty to treat prayers and giving of thanks or holy meditation about God's love, compassion, righteousness, etc., in a frivolous and improper manner?[7]

It is hardly necessary to offer the reminder that, just as solemnity has little in common with lethargy, one must not confuse a dignified pace with a dragging, crawling along.[8]

It is hardly possible to give a definite rule concerning how fast or slow a chorale melody should be sung, but it is determined not only by the different content of the songs, but also by the established custom in a given place and the existing sensitivity of an assembled congregation. In deep grief the tempo will instinctively be somewhat slower than at a time less depressing; at times of great joy the singing will take on a quicker, more spirited pace than will be the case with a more moderate joyfulness, even without the congregation especially attempting to do so. As a general rule it can only be suggested that one should always seek to accommodate the tempo of the singing to the true character of the song. Most of the time the precentor or organist has it entirely in his power to set the tempo in which the song is to be sung. If he understands his craft, he can with the first notes determine the character in which the congregation will instinctively sing the entire song.

Entirely improper and extremely out of place in hymn singing is the disfiguring of a melody with ornaments and so-called embellishments.[9] These sound especially repugnant when entire congregations strive to imitate the precentor and can hardly sing one note of the melody without adding to it one or two notes before and after. At most, an organist with good taste may now and then be permitted—when he does not have to fear thereby to corrupt the singing of his congregation and mislead it to embellish the singing—a proper ornament where it can contribute something to the beautifying of the whole, but never the singers of a chorale melody. Simplicity is one of the main beauties of our church's hymn singing, and in this we stand closer to the original singing in the assemblies of Christian worship than any other kind of Christian institution which has introduced other kinds of melodies beside hymn singing. The more simply a chorale is sung, the more beautiful it sounds. In the singing of a chorale not one single note should be heard, at least not in the melody, that is not specifically notated in the chorale book.

If singers are found in a congregation who possess such a good ear that they are able to sing an accurate bass part or inner voice to the melody, they may well put this talent to use in public singing, for it beautifies the singing of the congregation exceedingly.[10] Only it must always be done according to the prescribed harmony in the chorale book, otherwise instead of harmony the most unpleasant dissonance can arise. In congregations where a regular choir leads the singing, the entire congregation will gradually become used to harmonically correct singing; where no such choir is available or cannot be formed, the school teacher, singing with the children in school, can contribute in various ways to awaken in this or that child a hidden talent for singing that is harmonically correct.

In a hymn the congregation should follow the precentor.[11] From this it naturally follows that the precentor must never permit himself anything in his singing that he does not wish to see the congregation repeat or imitate. He must regard himself in all things as the congregation's model for singing, and for that reason give scrupulous attention that in every regard he is a good model. He must therefore:

1. Sing each melody definitely, with a clear, yet not too loud, voice and exactly according to the chorale book, so that the congregation can clearly perceive each note and can learn from him;

2. Abstain entirely from all embellishments and ornamentations;

3. Pronounce the words of the text clearly and without any additional strange letters;

4. Pay attention to the context of the song in order to begin fittingly, that is, neither too fast nor too slow, neither too loudly nor too softly;

5. Show in his bearing and entire demeanor that his heart and soul is filled with devotion and that he is conscious of performing his service before the eyes of God.

The organ should not lead the singing, but rather support it and keep it in better order; it is not the master but rather a humble servant in God's house. Organ playing in worship is not the end but the means. From this the following observations arise concerning the organists who have to accompany the singing of a congregation on the organ, which they would do well to heed.

Everything that is not suitable for the actual purpose of the gathering should be scrupulously avoided, and only the suitable manner of playing be chosen. The organist, therefore, cannot play well unless he himself is permeated with the importance of the actual purposes of the assembly. He must not be permitted to play according to his fancy, but his playing must measure up to the mood which the congregation is expecting to experience at the particular occasion. In large part his art depends on this, that he has sufficient means at his command to serve every purpose. He must be able to play brilliantly in order to put the congregation into a mood of festive, exultant joy; he must know how to bring forth soft, pensive melodies of melancholy when it is necessary to fill the hearts of the congregation with this feeling; he must be able to present in music the expression of holy, heavenly devotion in order that the souls of his hearers may, through his playing, be carried away to heaven. If the skill of an organist is not just too great, but perhaps only very ordinary, and if in general he is not in a position to attain the highest degree of suitable playing, he can still be expected to have the ability not to play too unsuitably; for example, not to play too loudly when he should play softly, not to play runs or roulades where they do not belong, not to play sadly at an occasion where he should arouse happy feelings, etc. Many an organist with little acquired skill contributes more to the edification of the congregation than another who is equipped with all possible intellectual learning and mechanical dexterity of his fingers, yet does not understand how to employ this at the appropriate places.

Perhaps it is not without value to draw several more specific rules from the preceding general observations concerning organ playing in the worship service and to recommend them to the attention of the organists.

1. The prelude with which the organist opens a service should always be calculated to awaken in the ears of the worshipers the feelings that should fill their hearts during this assembly, above all, therefore, the feeling of devotion. Devotion, however, has different subspecies, for example, joyful devotion, sad devotion, etc. And the prelude of the organist must seek to prepare the congregation for the particular kind of devotion for which the particular assembly is intended.

2. Certainly this is valid also in reference to the shorter preludes that are used to introduce the singing of the different hymns or single stanzas;[12] these also must be in the character of the hymn or verse which they should serve to introduce.

3. The interludes between the lines by no means have the purpose of providing an opportunity for the organist to demonstrate the dexterity of his fingers; rather they should

constitute an appropriate transition from one line to another, and serve as an introduction at the beginning of the next following line.[13] They must not be too long, allowing only sufficient time for the singers to take a new breath for the next line. In order to be fitting, they must harmonize not only with the overall character of the hymn or stanza but also with the sense and feeling of the preceding and following lines, yet without hesitation. Through well-chosen interludes the organist has an unbelievable power over the singing and the feeling of the congregation.

4. It is detrimental to the fine singing of a congregation when the organist is permitted to play harmonies other than those prescribed in the chorale book. Those singers who like to sing a bass or inner part to the melody either lose courage through such arbitrary changes or, if they continue singing according to the usual harmony while the organist plays an unusual one, there is naturally a disagreeable dissonance that destroys the good effect of the singing. In this instance, the organist must be willing, therefore, to disavow his art for the common good.

In conclusion, the editors of this work add the heartfelt wish that the chorale book itself, as well as the ideas just now set forth concerning good congregational singing and the excellent means for the achievement of this wish, may contribute something toward the desire to promote uniform and fine singing in all of our congregations in this western land, pleasing to the Lord in the assemblies of worship. May the Lord Himself, to whose honor our singing and playing resounds, bless our weak efforts for this important purpose and sanctify to himself the talents and means which He has given every member of our congregations to promote His praise through song and music.

> May He dwell among our songs of praise,
> Which we in weakness offer here below,
> In the future, as in the past, with His approval,
> Until one day our voices shall in purer choirs
> To honor God and the Lamb, who purchased us,
> United in the song of countless throngs
> In everlasting harmony, (together then) with all
>   the heavenly hosts
> Sound forth enraptured with the "Holy, holy, holy."

Notes

[1]The matter was first addressed in 1794 when the Pennsylvania Ministerium resolved that "Dr. Helmuth, F. A. Muhlenberg, Esq., and Mr. Moller of Philadelphia, be a committee to publish in German papers a plan for the publication of a tune book, in order that other preachers who have had experience in such work may express their opinions as to how such a useful book is to be best arranged; and that then the said committee proceed with the publication" (*Documentary History of the Pennsylvania Ministerium*, p. 270). No further mention of the committee or its activity is made until 17 years later. By this time both F. A. Muhlenberg (1750–1801), second son of H. M. Muhlenberg and noted for his political activities, and John Christopher Moller (1765–1803), German-born composer, organist, recitalist, and publisher who served as organist of St. Michael-Zion Lutheran Church in Philadelphia from 1790 to 1794, had died. In 1811 the minutes of the Ministerium record that "Dr. Helmuth reported concerning a (new) 'Choralbuch' which was to be printed in Philadelphia, and to contain 220 tunes for our Hymn Book, and wished that it might be generally introduced into all our congregations. The Synod, for its part, promised heartily to support it, in case the corporation of the Evangelical Lutheran congregation in Philadelphia retained the copyright" (*Documentary History*, p. 430). Just who the "venerable and very skillful musician" was cannot be ascertained with any certainty.

[2]The *Erbauliche Liedersammlung* was first published in 1786.

[3]The exact number of melodies was 266, with figured bass.

[4]Johann Balthasar Koenig's *Harmonischer Liederschatz oder allgemeines Evangelisches Choral-Buch*, Frankfort.,1738.

[5]Christian Gregor's *Choralbuch*, Leipzig, 1784; Justin Heinrich Knecht's *Vollstaendige Sammlung*, Stuttgart, 1799; and Johann Gottfried Vierling's *Choralbuch*, Cassel, 1789. Each of these books contained melody with figured bass.

[6]The American "singing school" movement that began in the early1700s in New England, made its way into Pennsylvania in James Lyon's *Urania* (l761) and in the publications of Andrew Adgate's Uranian Academy, 1785–88. By 1800 more than 130 tune books had been published in America for use by such singing schools. Several of William Billings' collections date from the 1770s.

[7]The emphasis on the stately, somber, and slow execution of the music through which means the singer or listener was able to absorb what was useful in the text was typical of the pietistic emphasis on music as a means of stirring up feelings of devotion. For pietism the simple hymn style, sung slowly and devotionally, was the best vehicle for this type of edification.

[8]The notoriously slow pace at which hymns were sung at this time, both on the Continent and in America, is well known and widely commented on. That it continued to be a problem throughout the 1880s is frequently reflected in the chorale book prefaces and in contemporary accounts of the time.

[9]*Schnoerkeleyen und sogenannte Verzierungen*. The practice of adding various embellishments to the hymn melody varied from the filling in of intervals with passing notes to such extreme examples as that given by Robert M. Stevenson in *Protestant Church Music in America* (New York, l966), p. 27. It was apparently a custom that persisted longer in the more rural regions.

[10]Such singing in parts must of necessity have been done "by ear," since the chorale book gave only the melody with figured bass.

[11]This custom of "lining out" the hymn was a necessity where no accompanying instrument such as the organ was available. That it brought with it several undesirable features is clear from the strictures that followed in the text.

27

[12]Short interludes, or *Zwischenspiele*, were frequently played between the various hymn stanzas. Various collections of such interludes became very popular among the German Lutherans in America throughout the 1800s.

[13]Interludes even between the lines of a single stanza indicate the extent to which the hymn stanzas were broken up, and underscore the matter of the slowness with which these stanzas undoubtedly were sung.

3

A Hymn
and Prayer-Book[1]

John Christopher Kunze's A Hymn and Prayer Book: for the Use
of Such Lutheran Churches as Use the English Language *(1795)*
was the first English Lutheran hymnal published in America.
Kunze, the son-in-law of Henry Melchior Muhlenberg, was deeply
concerned about the development of an English-speaking
Lutheranism in America. The hymns in this collection were taken
largely from the Psalmodia Germanica, *a Moravian collection, and*
hymns of Watts, Wesley, and Newton.

A Hymn and Prayer-Book

For the use of such Lutheran Churches
as use the English Language

Collected by John C. Kunze,[2] D.D.[3]
Senior of the Lutheran Clergy in the State of New
York

Col. 3: 16. Teaching and admonishing one another in
Psalms.

New York. Printed and sold by Hurtin and
Commardinger.
No. 450, Pearl Street (with privilege of Copy
Right.) 1795

Preface

The German churches in America have always been endeavoring to keep up their language, and have never neglected the proper means for this purpose. They have erected schools everywhere, and they catechize their children in German. These endeavors take place neither in contempt of the language prevailing in this part of the world, nor of the other Protestant religious societies, but in the nature of things. Parents arrive in this country without a competent knowledge of the English. They either find German churches established, or they come in such numbers to a place as to be able to establish them. There is then no question about the language. But the entrance of any religious society is connected with an implicit engagement to be and remain a supporter of it. I know of no authority commissioned to discharge any one from this obligation, except the interference of conscientious scruples about the salubrity of the doctrine. Any other consideration that ever induced a person to break up the membership with a congregation, was a violation of honesty, for such membership is founded in a contract.

From these two circumstances, the use of the German language and the obligation spoken of, the Germans find no inconvenience in most parts of the United States, where they have found such congregational union. But in some parts a difficulty begins to appear, and this is in populous cities, where their number is small, and in some country districts, where their settlements are mixed with English people. Here the children of the German parents, being not in the least aided by any German conversation in common life, and in some places not even enjoying an uninterrupted church service every Sunday, do not find the means supplied by the schools, which teach the German, sufficient to render the German church service useful to them. The result of this observation is not with us, that they must quit their connection, this would be a moral impossibility for the most of them. For they have, at their confirmation, entered the solemn promise of faithfulness as long as they find the doctrine consonant with Scripture: but that the use of the English in such places and congregations ought to be connected with the German, and this both in the church and school, as the French Hugenots do in all chief cities in Germany, with the French and the Germans. As this has been done already in some Lutheran congregations in New Jersey, and in this state, this little collection is intended to be offered to the evangelical brethren for their use in the above–mentioned purposes, in case it meets their approbation.[4]

Most all of the hymns are translations from the German,[5] and were used before in their churches. All except those in the appendix[6] are taken from printed books, particularly the German Psalmody,[7] printed in London and reprinted at New York, by H. Gaine, 1756, with which many serious English persons have been greatly delighted; and from an excellent collection of the Moravian brethren, printed in London, 1789.[8] In the appendix only I have taken the liberty to add a few of my own, and of the Reverend Messrs. Ernst's[9] and Strebeck's, both translations and original compositions.

The translation of the Liturgy, Catechism, and Order of Salvation is done by my worthy assistant in preaching, Mr. Strebeck,[10] and the rest added by myself, except the Prayers, which are taken from Joe. Alleine's excellent little work, "An Alarm to Unconverted Sinners." It was the intention, likewise, to add the Augustan Confession, and Mr. Strebeck has actually translated it from the Latin. But a disinclination to swell the size of the book was at this time preponderating. It is however ready, and can, at the desire of any one, who would not spare the expenses, be printed singly.

May the adorable Lord and Master, whose church has always been used and inclined to sing his praises, and who inhabits the praises of his Israel, deign these endeavors of a portion of his blessings, that with this little book in the hand and the contents in the heart, many souls, families, and congregations may worship him in the beauty of holiness.

J. C. Kunze

Notes

[1]The complete contents included 220 hymns (see n.6), Muhlenberg's liturgy of 1786 (trans. from the German by Georg Strebeck), the Gospels and Epistles, Luther's Small Catechism, Fundmentals of Theology, Starke's "Order of

Salvation" (trans. by Wrangel), A Table of Christian Duties, A Short Account of the Christian Religion, A Short Account of the Lutheran Church, Seven Penitential Psalms, and Prayers for Sunday and Weekdays.

[2]John Christopher Kunze (Aug. 5, 1744–July 24, 1807) was born at Artern on the Unstrut, Saxony; educated at Halle (under G. A. Francke), Rossleben, Merseburg, and the U. of Leipzig. Began his pastoral work in Philadelphia in 1770 as coadjuter of H. M. Muhlenberg at St. Michael and Zion Congregations. In 1771 he married Muhlenberg's second daughter (Margaretta Henrietta), and succeeded Muhlenberg as chief pastor in 1779. In 1773 he started a *Seminarium* in Philadelphia for the training of native pastors, which closed in 1776 because of the Revolutionary War. In 1784 Kunze accepted a call to New York where in the same year he united the old Dutch Church (Trinity) and the German Lutheran Church (Christ) into the United German Lutheran Churches in the city of New York. Kunze organized the New York Ministerium in 1786 and became the first president, continuing in office until his death. His *A Hymn and Prayer Book* (1795) was the first English language Lutheran hymnal published in America. Kunze was one of the most eminent scholars of his day, a specialist in oriental languages. In 1779, together with Thomas Jefferson, Anthony Wayne, and George Washington, Kunze was elected a member of the American Philosophical Society.

[3]Received in 1783 from the U. of Pennsylvania at the same time a D. D. degree was awarded to H. M. Muhlenberg, his father-in-law, and an honorary Doctor of Laws degree was awarded to George Washington. A personal notation in H. M. Muhlenberg's diary records Kunze's apology to his father-in-law for having been awarded this degree at the same time, considering himself unworthy to receive the degree at the same time as the eminent Pastor Muhlenberg.

[4]Kunze's ardent advocacy of the use of English in the church's worship when he was in Philadelphia for a time alienated his colleague Helmuth. This was undoubtedly involved in his decision to accept the call to New York in 1784. In New York Kunze set about to reintroduce English services begun as early as 1751 by Muhlenberg and continued by his successor Weyland, but dropped sometime before Kunze appeared on the scene. Kunze himself tried to preach in English, but soon gave it up because he found it too difficult. It was about a decade later when an available candidate who could preach in English appeared on the scene—George Strebeck.

[5]144 of the 239 hymns in this collection are translations, about half from the *Psalmodia Germanica* and half from an English Moravian collection. The remainder were of English origin, chiefly by Watts, Wesley, and Newton.

[6]The appendix contained 15 hymns, 6 of Kunze, 3 of Strebeck, and 4 of J. F. Ernst.

[7]*Psalmodia Germanica* or, *The German Psalmody*. Translated from the High Dutch. Together with their proper tunes, and thorough Bass (Third edition, corrected and very much enlarged; London, Printed: New York, reprinted and sold by H. Gaine, at the Bible and Crown, in Queen Street, 1756). The translations in this work were apparently the work of John Christian Jacobi, keeper of the Royal German St. James Chapel in London. Robin A. Leaver notes that this third edition was actually printed in 1765, the last two digits of the date having been inadvertently reversed. See *The Hymnal 1982 Companion*. Vol. Two. Raymond F. Glover, general editor. New York: The Church Hymnal Corporation, 1994, p. 488.

[8]*A Collection of Hymns*, for the use of the Protestant Church of the United Brethren. London printed: and sold at the Brethren's chapels, MDCCLXXXIX.

[9]Rev. J. F. Ernst was a pastor from the Albany region.

[10]Georg Strebeck was brought up as a Lutheran in Baltimore, Md., but later became a Methodist preacher. Anxious, so he claimed, for service in the

Lutheran Church, he was called as assistant pastor to Kunze in 1794 and ordained in 1796 by the New York Ministerium. The same year Strebeck became pastor of Zion Church in New York, the first English-speaking congregation in America formed out of Kunze's German congregation. A few years later Strebeck carried the bulk of his congregation over to the Protestant Episcopal Church.

4

A Collection
of Evangelical Hymns[1]

Early collections of hymns intended to serve Lutherans in America included English collections by George Strebeck, Ralph Williston, and two collections—one in German, one in English—by Paul Henkel. Three of these short Prefaces are given here. While none of these collections had a lasting impact, the two English collections, particularly, reflect the beginnings of the anglicizing of Lutheran hymnody that was to reach its peak in the later years of the 19th century.

A Collection of Evangelical Hymns

Made from Different Authors and Collections
For the English Lutheran Church in New York[2]
By George Strebeck[3]

and when they had sung a Hymn, they went out into the Mount of Olives. Mat. xxvi, 30

New York: Printed by John Tiebout, (Homer's Head) no. 358, Pearl Street, 1797

Advertisement

As this small collection of Hymns is published for the use of my own congregation, and by its peculiar request, it needs no apology.

The unsuitableness of the metres of our English Lutheran Hymn Book,[4] published in 1795, by Messrs. Hurtin and Commardinger, under the inspection of the Reverend Dr. Kunze, made it peculiarly necessary to provide another collection for the use of the English Lutheran Church. In the present collection I have endeavored to retain as many of the Hymns published in the former, as could well be done.[5] All those have this mark * prefixed to them; for the rest I am indebted to various authors,[6] and collections of reputation.[7] I hope none will be so bigotted to *mere name*, as to censure us for making selections from authors of this description, as may now be seen from the author's name being annexed to the Hymns.[8]

With regard to the performance of the present collection, I have only to say, I am sorry it is no better. The shortness of the time in which it was under contemplation, together with various avocations prevented my bringing it to such order and perfection, as might have been obtained under different circumstances. A few trivial mistakes have been discovered since the sheets have passed thro' the press, which I hope the kind reader will excuse.

It was the original design to have added a few more Hymns; but those already merited, seemed to swell the Volume to a size, which, considering the matter it is yet to contain, made me conclude it inconvenient to admit anymore. Such as the Collection is, I dedicate it to my brethren, to whom all my ministrations are cheerfully devoted; and pray that it may tend to their spiritual improvement.

George Strebeck New York, September, 1797

Notes

[1]The collection contained 304 hymns.

[2]Zion Church, New York was formed out of J. C. Kunze's German congregation in 1796, the year of Strebeck's ordination as the pastor of the first English-speaking Lutheran congregation in America. A few years later Strebeck and most of his congregation joined the Protestant Episcopal Church.

[3]See "A Hymn and Prayer-Book," J. C. Kunze, n. 10.

[4]Kunze's *A Hymn and Prayer-Book*.

[5]Of the 220 hymns in Kunze's *Hymn and Prayer-Book*, Strebeck retained 48, only ten of which are translations from the German.

[6]Of the remaining 236 hymns not taken from Kunze's *A Hymn and Prayer Book*, approximately half are from Isaac Watts and his school, about one-fifth from Charles Wesley, and about one-eighth from the "Olney Hymns."

[7]The specific collections referred to are not known.

[8]Strebeck here anticipates the objections of some who would note the departure of this book from traditional Lutheran contents.

5

A Choice Selection of Evangelical Hymns

From various Authors:
For the use of the English Evangelical Lutheran Church in New York[1]
By Ralph Williston[2]

I will sing with the Spirit, and I will sing with the understanding, also. 1 Cor. xiv. 13.

New York: Printed and sold by J. O. Totten; No. 155 Chatham-Street, 1806

The Evangelical Lutheran Ministry of this state having entered a resolution[3] some years ago, *That a new edition of the English Lutheran Hymn-Book should be procured*, and having left the selection of the Hymns to the members of their body residing in the City of New York: this collection is now offered to the public and public edification of such of our brethren, in religious connection with us as find the English language a necessary vehicle of assisting and promoting spiritual devotion.[4] The collection has been made by the Reverend Ralph Williston, Minister of the English Lutheran Church of this city, and I have examined and read every one of the Hymns now offered, before their being struck off, and can assure my fellow-worshippers, that none is found among them dissonant to our doctrine, or incompatible with the spirit of genuine godliness.

John C. Kunze, Senior of the Lutheran Clergy
in the State of New York
New York, February 20, 1806

Advertisement

Dear Brethren,

Through the solicitation of the Board of Trustees and Vestry of the English Evangelical Lutheran Zion Church, you are here presented with a choice selection of Evangelical Hymns, suited to private, family, social and public worship. These Hymns, are selected from various authors[5] of the first reputation and celebrity. It is not pretended that a Hymn will be found here, adapted to every religious subject, yet it is hoped there will be no important deficiency. No doctrine, it is believed, will be found in this selection, which is not accordant with the doctrines taught in our church.[6] A new edition, or a new compilation, became indispensably necessary, there not being a single copy to be had of the former collection:[7] and the obvious deficiency of the former collection, determined us to make a new compilation. Such as the present selection is, it is dedicated to you, as a testimony of affection; exhorting you to "Sing with the spirit, and with the understanding also." May it please Almighty God, to make it a means of assisting the praise, and promoting the edification of the church.

Ralph Williston New York
March, 1806

Notes

[1]The remainder of Zion Church, New York, which had not gone over to the Protestant Episcopal Church with its former pastor, Georg Strebeck.

2Ralph Williston was Georg Strebeck's successor at Zion Church, becoming its pastor in 1805. Originally a Methodist, Williston later followed Strebeck by reincorporating the only English Lutheran Church in New York as Zion Protestant Episcopal Church in 1810.

3In 1803 the New York Ministerium appointed a committee of J. C. Kunze, F. H. Quitman, and Georg Strebeck "to collect and print a hymnbook in the English language for our congregations in this state." This was apparently to be an official hymnbook of the New York Ministerium. The minutes of the Ministerium in the years immediately following contain no report of the committee's work, if indeed there was any.

4With Strebeck's defection to the Episcopal Church and no apparent activity on the part of the other members of the committee (Quitmann and Kunze) toward implementing the New York Ministerium resolution of 1803, it may be that it was felt that Williston's volume would fit the need. In spite of Kunze's endorsement, however, there is no indication that this was an official product endorsed by the New York Ministerium.

5The hymns of Isaac Watts and Charles Wesley make up about three-fourths of the book. The rest are from other evangelical writers. Among the Passion hymns seven are taken from Kunze's book.

6In spite of this certification, Benson (*The English Hymn*, 1915, reprint of 1962, p. 413) suggests that "neither its arrangements nor contents suggests Lutheranism."

7Indicative of the short life and relative lack of influence of Strebeck's volume of 1797.

6

Das Neu eingerichtete Gesangbuch

bestehend Aus der Sammlung der besten Liedern, zum Gebrauch des oeffentlichen Deutschen Gottes- diensts, und anderen ¨Übungen zur Gottseligkeit, in den Vereinigten Staaten, von Nord-America

Erste Auglage. Neu-Market, Gedruckt: bei Ambro- sius Henkel und Comp., 1810

The Newly Arranged Hymnbook

Consisting of a Collection of the Best Songs for Use in Public German Worship Services and in Other Exercises Toward Godliness in the United States of North America

First Edition[1], New Market, Published by Ambrosius Henkel and Company[2], 1810

Foreword

Kind Christian Reader:

Here you have a small hymnbook which has been written and arranged with all possible care, so that it may be useful to you in public worship and on other worship occasions. We have prepared this book because we know that before this time some people who had no hymnbooks and others who were indifferent brought no hymnbooks to church and, therefore, the preachers found it necessary to lead the hymns in church by intonation and response.[3] The result was that some weren't at all concerned about getting hymn-books for their households. Thus even fewer hymnbooks came to the people through purchase (especially in our state).[4]

But nevertheless, many concerned and well-intentioned people desire that the use of hymnbooks, as in the past, again be introduced. They probably recognize that when hymnbooks aren't used in the church, they are also used little at home, especially by the young, and thus the young are neither trained in singing nor receive the instruction they would from the use of the hymnbooks.[5] So we found it necessary to edit and publish this little hymnbook, a practical and convenient book to carry in the pocket for church worship and small in cost, compared to the price of other hymnbooks. We know that people often justifiably complain about both points. We have collected only as many songs as we regarded necessary for use in an orderly worship service.[6] We have also chosen only songs that can be sung according to familiar melodies.[7] In addition, the very long songs have not been retained totally, since in the public worship they are never sung in their entirety anyway.[8]

The many spiritually rich and edifying songs that are found in various hymnbooks, books which some people have, still can be profitably read and considered at home. This hymnbook, however, we have so edited and arranged that it can be used generally in the public worship service.

Those who would choose on some occasion to use the hymns in intonation and response will find that especially convenient in this book as they soon will see by the arrangement.

The fact that one or more songs are prescribed according to

the content of the so-called Gospel for each Sunday and also for each ordinary festival day throughout the entire year is not intended to compel anyone to preach on the basis of the Gospel text, as is the practice with some. That is only for those who choose to do so. Every competent teacher will surely see that the songs so arranged certainly are suitable for many other Scripture passages and texts as well and can be used with them.

This little hymnbook consists of a collection of the best and most usable songs that we could find in the various available hymnbooks. Also it was necessary to add some hymns that were not found in other books, so that one may have useful songs for every circumstance.

This book is also arranged as much as possible so that every responsible teacher can make use of it in all his official ministries. We also hope that it may be read, sung, and considered by all Christians at all opportunities to the glory of God and to the edification of their own souls and the souls of others. That is the sincere wish of the publisher and those who share the work with him.

Paul Henkel,[9] Evangelical Preacher
New Market, Shenandoah County, Virginia, 1810

Notes

[1]The first edition was published in 1810.

[2]The Henkel Printing Company was begun by Paul Henkel and his sons Solomon H. and Ambrose at New Market, Virginia. Involved in missionary work west of the Allegheny mountains, they published a variety of religious material which they needed for their work among the various congregations, including an edition of the Book of Concord (1851) and Luther's Large and Small Catechisms (1854).

[3]"*Die Gesaenge in der Kirche vorzusprechen.*" The pastor or cantor would intone and sing the hymn, line by line, to which the congregation responded by imitating the line just heard. (See also the description in the introduction to the *Choral-Buch für die Erbauliche Liedersammlung der Deutschen Evangelisch–Lutherischen Gemeinen in Nord-Amerika.* Philadelphia. 1813.)

[4]The editor is obviously not unmindful of the commercial aspects of the situation.

[5]Reference is to the teaching function of hymnody which, in Lutheranism, was of equal importance to its musical value. The arrangement of the hymns was frequently didactic. Often the various hymn–books included Luther's Small Catechism, prayers, psalms, Gospel lessons, and the like.

[6]The first edition of 1810 contained 246 hymns; the second edition of 1812 included three additional ones.

[7]The melody listing suggests 25 classes or metrical patterns. The book contained only texts.

[8]Because of the length of the hymns and because the melodies of the pietistic period took on the isometric style that encouraged a slower and dragging style of singing, hymns with many stanzas became laborious and time-consuming to use. It became common to delete some stanzas.

[9]Paul Henkel (1754–1825), the great home missionary of the early 19th century, came from a long line of pastors, his great-grandfather, Anthony Jacob Henkel, being regarded as the founder of the old Lutheran churches in Philadelphia and Germantown. Paul Henkel took part in the organization of the North Carolina Synod in 1803, and later of the Ohio Synod in 1818 and the Tennessee Synod in 1820. He and his five sons—Phillip, Ambrose, Andrew, David, and Charles—were all pastors well-known for their orthodoxy. In general this hymnal was an undistinguished collection. It was most probably used only by a relatively small number of congregations.

7

A Collection of Hymns, and a Liturgy[1]

A Collection of Hymns, and a Liturgy appeared in 1814 as the official hymnal of the New York Ministerium. It was primarily the work of Frederick H. Quitman, president of the Ministerium and an avowed rationalist, and is characterized by its almost complete rejection of the Lutheran chorale heritage, turning instead almost exclusively to English sources, by its alteration of hymn texts to conform to the rationalistic tendency of the time, and by its aversion to any prescribed liturgy.

A Collection of Hymns, and a Liturgy

For the use of Evangelical Lutheran Churches;
To which are added Prayers for Families and
Individuals

Published by Order of the Evangelical Lutheran
Synod of the State of New York

"I will pray with the spirit, and I will pray with
the understanding also. I will sing with the spirit.
and I will sing with the understanding also."
I Cor. 14: 15.

Philadelphia
Printed and sold by G. and D. Billmeyer
1814

Preface

The singing of hymns is justly considered a delightful and important part of public worship. It was in use even among the ancient heathens. Moses introduced it, by divine command into his religious institution; and David raised it to high perfection by his poetical talents and musical skill. Our blessed Saviour has recommended this pious exercise to his followers by his own practice; and St. Paul exhorts us to "teach and admonish one another in spiritual songs, singing with grace in our hearts to the Lord." No act of social religion is either more pleasing in itself, or more happily adapted to cherish the love of God and man, than that which is enforced by these high authorities.

The Lutheran church in Germany is distinguished for its attachment to sacred music, and is possessed of, perhaps, the best and most numerous collections of hymns extant in the Christian world. From this source, our congregations in the United States have derived abundant supplies. The prevalence of the English language, however, makes it necessary for many members of our communion to conduct their public worship, altogether, or in part, in that language, and of course to provide for them a compilation of English hymns. This has indeed been already attempted by several individuals.[2] But as the selections, published by them, evidently admit of great improvement,[3] another was ordered to be prepared by a committee[4] appointed for that purpose by the Lutheran Synod of the State of New York, convened at Rhinebeck in September A.D. 1812;[5] and, in compliance with this order, the following work is printed. It is not pretended to be as perfect as could be wished, nor are all its parts of equal value, but the materials, of which it is composed, have been chosen with no little care and consideration; a large number of hymn-books of various denominations has been consulted; and it is hoped, that it will receive in a good degree the approbation of those for whom it is intended, and become a means of promoting their edification.

The same committee[6] was charged with the preparation of a new and enlarged Liturgy for our churches.[7] Forms of prayer, with necessary directions and addresses to congregations, are accordingly, presented in this volume, proper to be employed in divine service generally, in the administration of the sacraments, and in the celebration of other solemn rites customary amongst us. But the use of these forms is left entirely to the discretion of congregations and ministers, the Synod having no design to make them binding upon any in connection with us, but judging that the leaders of the devotions of their brethren should be at perfect liberty to address the throne of grace in their own words. It will, perhaps, be found most expedient, that such forms and the free or precomposed prayers of ministers should be used alternately. At all events, the Liturgy will, we trust, prove serviceable to young clergymen, to vacant churches, and to persons remote from Christian temples and desiring to unite together in the adoration of the most High.

Along with devotional exercises for congregations, it has been thought proper to publish others for families and individuals, adapted to a variety of situations, relations, and characters. Some of these, as well as several parts of the Liturgy, have been translated from the German; others have been taken from English authors and collections; and a considerable degree of freedom has been used in selecting and framing them. We commend this part of the work particularly to the attention of our brethren in their domestic and private worship; believing, that it breathes a spirit of pure Christian piety and love; and hoping, that it will assist in instructing the young and uninformed how to pray, in comforting the distressed, in awakening a sense of religion in the careless, and in quickening the faith, hope, and charity of upright believers in the Lord Jesus Christ.

To the whole of this book, as far as it agrees with his truth in scripture, may it please Almighty God to give his blessing, and make it instrumental in glorifying his name.

FREDERICK H. QUITMANN,[8] D. D.
President of the Evangelical Lutheran Synod
of the State of New York.

AUGUSTUS WACKERHAGEN,[9] Secretary, t

Notes

[1]The collection contained 520 hymns, A Liturgy for the Use of Evangelical Lutheran Churches (containing a variety of worship orders and related liturgical material), and a group of Prayers for the Use of Families and individuals. The arrangement of the hymns does not follow the church year.

[2]For example, the collections of J. C. Kunze (1795), Georg Strebeck (1797), and Ralph Williston (1806).

[3]Part of the "improvement" necessary, according to Quitmann, was to bring the hymnody in line with the more rationalistic tendency of the day. Luther Reed also notes that this book's "emphasis upon the ethical rather than the devotional was in agreement with the point of view and the practice of New England Unitarianism." (The Lutheran Liturgy, rev. ed., 1947, p. 176) Also the relative infelicity of the earlier translations of Kunze did little to reflect favorably upon the entire attempt to translate the German hymnody into English. Quitmann's own ability to handle the English language, clearly demonstrated in this Preface, could only have been repulsed by these earlier and cruder attempts.

[4]The members of the committee cannot be determined with certainty from the minutes of the Ministerium. However, an article on "English Lutheran Hymnbooks" (Evangelical Review, XI, October, 1859, 188) by William Reynolds states that the committee consisted of F. H. Quitmann, Augustus Wackerhagen, and Mayer (undoubtedly P. F. Mayer, pastor of St. John's Lutheran Church in Philadelphia and chairman of a committee which prepared the 1834 edition of this same hymnbook).

[5]This is an error. In 1812 the Ministerium did not meet. It was scheduled to meet in Koblesfill in September, but was prevented from doing so by the War of 1812. The resolution to produce an English hymnbook occurred at the synodical meeting in 1811 in Wurtemburgh, not in Rhinebeck in 1812 (See Nicum, Geschichte des New York Ministerium (p. 94).

[6]See note 4.

[7]Quitmann's Liturgy clearly reflects rationalistic and deistic leanings: the Lord's Supper became a "Memorial of Christ's death and a means of improving his disciples in their attachment and obedience to his divine religion;" God is referred to as "the great Parent of the Universe;" and other similar examples.

[8]Frederick Henry Quitmann (Aug. 7, 1760–June 26, 1832) was born in Iserloh, Germany. He studied at Halle under Johan Semler, the rationalist. Ordained in 1783 at the Lutheran Consistory in Amsterdam, Holland, he served the Dutch Lutheran Colony in Curacao. He came to the United States in 1795, serving several pastorates for more than 30 years, and served as second president of the New York Ministerium from 1807–1825. He was a well-educated and persuasive person, and a thorough-going rationalist. He "denied the authority of the Bible and Lutheran Confessions, and the liturgy and hymnal which he edited was decidedly un-Lutheran." (Gerhard Lenski, Encyclopedia of the Lutheran Church, Augsburg, 1965.)

[9]Augustus Wackerhagen (?–Nov. 1, 1865), Quitmann's son-in-law, was ordained in 1806 and followed his father-in-law as president of the New York Ministerium, serving from 1826–1829. He also served at various times as secretary and treasurer of the Ministerium.

8

Das Gemeinschaftliche Gesangbuch

The desire was frequently heard in the early 1800s for a "common book" which could serve both Lutheran and Reformed churches in America. Rationalism had tended to blur confessional differences and a "common book" often seemed the most prudent course in the common cause of evangelizing America. Also, since many Lutheran and Reformed churches shared the same building, a "common book" was a practical answer to providing a book both groups could use. Published on the 300th anniversary of the Reformation, Das Gemeinschaftliche Gesangbuch (1817)—together with Quitman's A Collection of Hymns, and a Liturgy (1814)—represent the low points of American Lutheran hymnody.

Das Gemeinschaftliche Gesangbuch

zum gottesdienstlichen Gebrauch der Lutherischen und Reformierten Gemeinden in Nord-America

1st Edition, Baltimore, Gedruckt und herausgegeben von Schaffer und Maund, 1817

The Common Hymn Book

For use in the worship of Lutheran and Reformed congregations in North America

First Edition, Baltimore, Printed and distributed by Schaffer and Maund, 1817

Preface

The salutary purpose of this book[1] is indicated clearly enough on the title page.[2] Where is there a family in our land that, to one degree or another, is not composed of members of both Lutheran and Reformed churches? How welcome a book of this kind must be in every household—a book which not only removes the difficulty that inevitably arises in the public worship of "common churches" from the use of two different books; but also provides an unusual heightening effect in home devotions, when the entire family, just as they read from one Bible, can also praise and laud their God and Savior from one hymnbook. At the same time this book has the purpose of breaking down the wall of partition between Lutherans and Reformed, which is based only on prejudice, and to spread abroad the true spirit of tolerance and brotherhood, and to unite one Christian with another ever more fervently.[3]

Concerning the arrangement of the book, it is most important to note that the doctrine and ethics of Jesus' religion have been divided into three main sections that are printed at the beginning of the book with a complete Table of Contents. For each section in the collection the most practical hymns have been chosen. Here everyone can obtain a better understanding of his faith and arrange his worship (at church or at home) in a more useful and God-pleasing manner, and here every preacher can choose edifying and fitting hymns for his public discourses.[4]

Besides this, it was the purpose of the editor[5] of this hymnbook to have a particularly practical arrangement, which was lacking in our previous hymnbooks. For while we are convinced that the esteemed men who provided for the publication of those earlier hymnbooks some 30 years ago have done much good under God's blessing,[6] we are just as certain that they would have arrived at a more practical arrangement if they had had the materials which we now have.

In accordance with these resources, we now submit that the hymnbooks published in the last 20 years depart from the older books in that they always place in the first section—which contains the dogmatic theology—the teachings concerning the knowledge of God, the creation, the attributes and perfections of God, the Fall and the sorry consequences thereof, and only then the teaching concerning the consoling salvation through Jesus Christ. We have chosen and retained this arrangement in place of the older one as a more practical one because it is entirely suited to the teaching of the Bible and is also suited to an orderly development of the knowledge of God and Jesus.

The contents of the headings in the first section remain what they were previously, only we have considered it necessary to make the arrangement more complete and have indicated this by specific additions in the outline. The headings in the second and third sections have been expanded and, as in the first section, properly arranged and the particular contents noted. Furthermore, since it is not the number of hymns in a hymnbook, but rather a good and suitable choice of hymns that provides the necessary completeness, we have in this present collection as much as possible given attention to the latter requirement. Nevertheless, there is such a complete number of hymns appointed that it has become possible to satisfy the principle set forth. The large number of the hymns have been taken from our old hymnals on both sides, especially those which have been commonly recognized and long used as edifying core hymns. They have been retained unchanged when they combined a spiritual content with a purity of expression. Several have been altered where the expression was obscure or was not appropriate, or where it would be prejudicial to edification and devotion. Those that lacked spirituality and grammatical correctness throughout were omitted. In the place of such old hymns which, because of their unknown meter, could never be sung in most churches, new hymns are given with known melodies whose authors are not only good poets but also practical and pious Christians, for example Lavater, Sturm, Gellert, Cramer, and others.[7] So also the name of the author, when it is known, is always prefixed to the hymn.

We have also had due regard for the melodies in order to make the book useful also for those regions that often lack a good song leader. In this connection it should be noted for the sake of those who lead in public singing that as far as melodies were concerned we followed the chorale book published in 1813 in Philadelphia for the *Erbauliche Liedersammlung*.[8] Also in assigning melodies we always chose those which, following the practice of the aforementioned chorale book, suit the content of the hymn. Where you find two melodies suggested above a hymn, it should be noted that the first is the more appropriate.

May God accompany this book with His benediction and through it effect a common edification and a true and efficacious Christianity, and may brotherhood, tolerance, and unity more and more be spread abroad. This is the heartfelt wish of the author as well as the publisher.[9]

Baltimore, January 1, 1817

Notes

[1]The hymnal contained 494 hymns, a small collection of prayers, and a listing of the Epistles and Gospels for the church year.

[2]It was intended chiefly for use by Lutheran and Reformed congregations who shared the same church building. Such "union churches" were common, and common hymnbooks the answer to a practical problem.

[3]The movement toward a union of Lutheran and Reformed churches was due in part to a spirit of religious indifference fostered by the inroads of rationalism, in part because it was often the line of least resistance, but also because it frequently appeared to be the most prudent course in the common cause of evangelism. Rationalism tended to obliterate confessional differences. Lutherans, Reformed, and other protestants in America were making joint plans to celebrate the 300th anniversary of the Reformation. The general climate at least was conducive to a variety of united activities.

[4]This was typical of the viewpoint prevalent at this time which, for the most part, relegated the hymn to underscoring the ideas of the preacher's "public discourses."

[5]While the preface is unsigned, it is clear that Frederick Quitman, at this time president of the New York Ministerium, played a large role in this hymnal's development and ultimate shape. The first edition carried the endorsement of August Wackerhagen, Dr. C. L. Becker, Daniel Kurz, F. D. Schaefer, and, most importantly, Frederick Quitmann, who praised its timeliness and urged its introduction into the parishes of his brethren.

[6]Muhlenberg's *Erbauliche Liedersammlung* was published 31 years earlier in 1786.

[7]Only one of Luther's hymns was included, 11 by Gerhardt, while Gellert, the leading writer of the Rationalistic period, was represented by 40. Luther Reed's evaluation suggests that "the incapacity of the editors was revealed not only in the omission of the classic hymns of the church and the insertion of weak and frivolous hymns, but also in the frequent errors in crediting authorship, etc." (*The Lutheran Liturgy*, p. 171).

[8]*Choral-Buch für die Erbauliche Liedersammlung der Deutschen Evangelisch-Lutherischen Gemeinden in Nord Amerika* (Philadelphia: Conrad Zentler and Georg Blake, 1813).

[9]Typical of the positive response of those attracted to such union efforts was that of Rev. G. Schober of the North Carolina Synod: "This meritorious undertaking paves the way to universal harmony, union, and love among our

Lutheran and Reformed Churches, removing all the obstacles which hitherto prevented that happy effect. . ." Less enthusiastic was the evaluation of Socrates Henkel: "No doubt, this insidious course produced, to a considerable extent, for the time being, the effect which the author of those lines [Schober] so much desired. . . . But whilst it was doing this, it was aiding in engendering and cultivating a spirit which. . . ultimately resulted in ignoring some of the most vital and fundamental doctrines and elements of the Church, leaving her in that latitudinarian state of indifference and laxness in regard to almost everything that was regarded as positive and definite. . . . a deplorable wreck, requiring years for its restoration" (Henkel, *History of the Evangelical Lutheran Tennesee Synod* (New Market: Henkel & Co., 1890), p. 6).

9

Hymns, Selected and Original, for Public and Private Worship[1]

The General Synod, a loose federation of Lutheran synods organized in 1820, produced two hymnals: its English Hymns, selected and original *(1828) and its German* Evangelische Liedersammlung *(1830). The chief architect of its English book was Samuel Simon Schmucker, a strong proponent of "American Lutheranism," a movement which argued for adapting Lutheranism to the American scene to make it more palatable in America. This collection also clearly reflects the influence of the Second Great Awakening which attempted to embody the full scope of the new evangelical theology and experience, the worship style, "new measures," and the hymns and songs of revivalism which was sweeping the country. The German book was largely a compilation from Muhlenberg's hymnbook of 1786 and the "Common Book" of 1817.*

Hymns, Selected and Original, for Public and Private Worship

Published by the General Synod of the Ev. Lutheran Church

Published Gettysburg, Pa. Stereotyped by L. Johnson Phila. 1828

Preface

Singing the praises of God is justly regarded as one of the most delightful and profitable parts of worship, both public and private. It was introduced by divine command into the worship of the Old Testament; the blessed Savior himself recommended it by his practice; and it is enjoined by the apostle Paul and Christians in general. Its separate utility, in addition to that of prayer and hearing the word of God, is based upon the very nature of the human mind, as it calls into action additional powers of the soul. Yet as the materials for the exercise of this Christian duty in any other than the Hebrew language, whether translations of the Psalms or original effusions on the doctrines and fact of the Scriptures, are necessarily the products of uninspired pens; they are characterized by different degrees of merit both in respect to poetic excellence and devotional tendency. In no other language, it is thought, is there extant so copious and excellent a collection of Psalms and hymns and Spiritual Songs, as that of the Lutheran Church in Germany. And from this copious source our German churches in this country have drawn ample supplies. Yet the prevalence of the English language has, in some places, long since led to its introduction into the service of our sanctuaries, as well as to the publication of several collections of hymns in the same tongue. Among these, that made by the learned and pious Dr. Kunze,[2] then Senior of the New York Ministerium, and published in 1795, is excellent in its devotional tendency, but lamentably deficient in poetic beauty and purity of diction. The collection, subsequently made by a Committee of the New York Synod,[3] appointed in 1812, not only merits a decided preference, but is indeed a most excellent work. Yet long experience has evinced that this selection does not afford a sufficient practice, and many of the choicest and most devotional productions of the English muse are not contained in it.

Under these circumstances, the General Synod deemed it their duty, in accordance with their Constitution, and in obedience to the numerous calls made on them, to provide a hymnbook possessing alike sufficient amplitude, classical excellence, and devotional spirit, to serve as a permanent book for the churches of their connection, and for all others who may be disposed to use it. For this purpose the undersigned were appointed a committee in 1825, and have for several years devoted their most particular and prayerful attention to the important duty assigned them. They have found the work arduous far beyond their early expectations; but their conviction of its importance and necessity has continually increased. Their aim has been to combine in the highest possible degree practical excellence with the charms and graces of poetry. They have procured all the most excellent and valuable hymnbooks used by sister churches, and have also examined very many hymns dispersed through the works of individual authors.[5] They feel assured that the selection made will contain the major part of the best hymns extant in the English language. They have also, after mature consideration, constructed a new arrangement,[6] which they deem decidedly more practical than any other which they have seen, and calculated to be more useful both to ministers and laymen.

A view of general subjects, sufficiently minute for reference, is prefixed to the book. A portable size was adopted, not only for the sake of cheapness and convenience in public and domestic worship, but also that Christians who strive to walk with God, and delight to sing the songs of Zion, may carry this volume with them on their journeys, and in their social walks, and into the field of labor, and as opportunity may offer, kindle anew the flame of their devotion at the fire of the sacred muse.

In conclusion, we would commend this work to the serious use of the disciples of our Lord in general, and our churches in particular; and more especially to the favor and blessing of that divine Redeemer, whose dying love will be the theme of our more perfect praises in the realms of celestial bliss.

S. S. Schmucker,[7] Professor of Theology
in the Theological Seminary of the General Synod
of the Evangelical Luth. Church
C. P. Krauth,[8]
Pastor of the Second English Lutheran Church,
Philadelphia
G. Shober,[9] Pastor of the Lutheran Church
Salem, North Carolina
J. G. Schmucker, D. D.,[10] Pastor of the Lutheran Church
York, Pennsylvania

B. Keller,[11] Pastor of the Lutheran Church
Germantown, Pennsylvania

Gettysburg, Pa., May 16, 1828

Preface to the New Edition[12]

Various changes in this Hymn book having been called for,[13] a committee was, at the meeting of the General Synod in 1845,[14] appointed to examine what was desirable in this respect, and directed to report to the Synod at its next meeting in the city of New York in 1848. The committee having done so, their report was accepted, and their number having been increased by the addition of one member from each Synod not already represented in that committee, they were directed to make the alterations and improvements indicated as necessary, and to have the book stereotyped and published.

The committee, consisting of 15, being too unwieldy and too widely separated for frequent consultation, having had a meeting during the session of the General Synod, and agreed upon a mode of action for the decision of one or two points, committed the details of the work to a sub-committee of three who resided in the same place, (Gettysburg, Pa.),[15] and could therefore perform the task assigned them with the greatest deliberation. The results of their labors are herewith presented to the church.

It is needless to specify in detail the changes that they have made, but they may state in general that, in accordance with the report and resolutions under which they were appointed, they carefully revised the text of the whole work, making such verbal changes as seemed necessary or desirable, removed some 50 of the most objectionable hymns from the body of the book as originally prepared, threw out all duplicates, substituted improved editions of hymns where they presented themselves, rejected such stanzas of hymns as seemed injurious to them, and rearranged the whole Appendix, from which they removed those hymns generally to which well grounded exception appeared to have been taken in our churches. For the hymns removed they, of course, substituted others, and without increasing the size or price of the book, have added some 40 others, so as to make the whole number of new hymns in this edition about 150.[16]

These changes, they believe, will generally commend themselves to those interested in this work. They might indeed have been carried further, but it was not contemplated that the book should be so remodeled as to be incapable of being used in connection with the previous editions. On a subsequent page will be found directions for the use of the new in connection with the old book, and the plan is so plain and simple that it is hoped that no inconvenience will be experienced in this respect.

To facilitate the use of hymns translated from the German,[17] of which as many as seemed desirable under existing circumstances have been introduced, a table of tunes suitable to them, or the melodies of their originals, the metres of which have been preserved, is appended.

No table of scriptural passages has been introduced, because very little use seems to be made of such tables, and because the few references that were made to such passages at the headings of hymns in former editions, have been omitted in this for the sake of brevity and of uniformity. It is hoped that a careful statement of the subject of each hymn, at its head, and a copious index of subjects[18] will supply all that is here needed.

Hoping that the book, thus revised and enlarged, will meet the wants and expectations of those for whom it is intended, and animate more and more the devotions of our churches and of individual Christians, and praying that all who use it may "sing with spirit and with understanding," and that the Triune God may accept the praises, and answer the prayers thus addressed unto Him, we herewith commit this volume to our ministers and people.

Committee of the General Synod

Wm. M. Reynolds,[19] Synod East Penna.
H. L. Baugher, Synod Maryland
S. S. Schmucker, Synod West Penna.
Chas. P. Schaeffer,[20] Synod New York
H. I. Schmidt, Synod Hartwick
L. Eichelberger, Synod Virginia

G. Scherer, Synod West'n Virginia
J. D. Scheck, Synod North Carolina
P. A. Strobel, Synod South Carolina
H. G. Keil, Synod Ohio, (English)
J. H. Hoffman, Synod Wittenberg
W. H. Harrison. Synod Miami
P. Springer. Synod Illinois
J. Winecoff, Synod Allegheny
P. Glenn, Synod South West

Notes

[1]The original edition of this book apparently did not list the sources for the hymns used. The revised edition, however, accompanies the alphabetical listing of hymns with a designation of sources. These sources indicate that "selected" materials far outnumber "original." There are included, however, at least two hymns of S. S. Schmucker, one of the members of the hymnal committee.

[2]John Christopher Kunze (1744–1807), was a German-American Lutheran pioneer pastor, scholar, and organizer. He came to America at the age of 26 and became a pastor in Pennsylvania and New York. In 1786, he succeeded in formally organizing the second Lutheran synod in America, the Ministerium of New York. He was a Hebrew scholar who taught Semitic languages at the University of Pennsylvania and at Columbia University (then Kings College). He sponsored and encouraged English preaching and worship and privately trained young men for the ministry who would become the first English Lutheran pastors in America. He was instrumental in translating the liturgy (published by the Pennsylvania Ministerium in 1786 into English) and published it along with a collection of English hymns entitled *A Hymn and Prayer Book, for the use of such Lutheran Churches as use the English language* (1795).

[3]In 1807, upon the death of J. C. Kunze, the presidency of the New York Ministerium passed for 21 years to Dr. Fred Henry Quitman who had come from Europe as an avowed disciple of Professor John Semler, "father of rationalism" at Halle. In 1812, Quitman prepared and published, with the consent and approval of the synod, an English catechism as a substitute for Luther's which denied the inspiration and authority of the Bible and the validity of the Apostles' Creed and the chief Lutheran confessions. He also endorsed a distinctly un-Lutheran liturgy and hymnal in 1817, entitled *Das Gemeinschaftliche Gesangbuch zum Gottesdienstlichen Gebrauch der Lutherischen und Reformirten Gemeinden in Nord-America.*

[4]See the *Minutes of the Proceedings of the General Synod of the Evangelical Lutheran Church in the United States* convened at Frederick, Md., October 1825, and the minutes of the General Synod convened at Gettysburg, Pa., October, 1827.

[5]Although no listing of sources is given in the first edition, the revised edition lists sources that might be considered representative for both. Names of individuals that occur frequently include the following; Addison, Beddome,

Collyer, Cowper, Doddridge, Kelly, Montgomery, Newton, Stennett, Toplady, J. Wesley and S. Wesley, Jr. C. Wesley is represented approximately 60 times and Watts has made almost 200 contributions. "Steele" is present 37 times and "Mrs. Steele" is given credit for 12 entries. "Collections" referred to include those of Aldridge, Campbell, Dobell, Leeds, Rippon, and many others. Also, reference is made to the New York Collection, Methodist Collection, Episcopal Collection, Baptist Psalmody, *Psalmodia Germanica*, Select Hymns, Village Hymns, and the Church Psalmody.

⁶The "Tabular View of Contents" in the edition of 1832 lists hymns in the following sections; I. The Scriptures, II. Being and Perfections of God, III. Trinity, IV. Praise to God, V. The Works of God, VI. Providence of God, VII. Fall and Depravity of Man, VIII. Christ, IX. Names and Characters of Christ, X. Holy Spirit, XI. The Gospel Call, XII. Penitence of the Awakened Sinner, XIII. Supplication for the Divine Mercy, XIV. Salvation Through Jesus Christ, XV. Christian Experience, XVI. The Means of Grace, XVII. Kingdom and Church of Christ, XVIII. Particular Occasions and Circumstances (including such subheadings as Spring, Summer, and Harvest, New Year, Birthday Hymns, and Meeting and Parting of Christian friends), XIX. Death, XX. Resurrection, XXI. Judgment, XXII. Eternity, and XXIII. Dismissions and Doxologies.

⁷Samuel Simon Schmucker (1799–1873) was the son of J. G. Schmucker. He was born in Hagerstown, Md., but at age 11 moved to York, Pa., where he attended the academy there. Subsequently he pursued classical studies at the University of Pennsylvania and theology at Princeton, since no Lutheran seminary was available. The Princeton experience purportedly had a profound effect on his theological views, which were quite ecumenical and humanistically oriented. In 1820 he was licensed as a pastor by the Pennsylvania Ministerium. In 1823 he is credited with saving the General Synod from dissolution and he remained a strong organizational leader from that time. In 1825 the synod referred the project of a new hymnbook to a committee with Schmucker as chairman. Three years later the book appeared in print as the first edition of *Hymns, selected and original.* Commenting on this book, Benson (*The English Hymn*, p. 417) says; "At the time the wave of rationalism was being succeeded by a wave of revivalism, and revival methods were replacing catechetical. The book is in full sympathy with the new methods, appropriating many rude revival songs. The textual treatment of the standard hymns is often distressing, and as containing the authorized hymnody of a historic Church, with its inherited standards of doctrine and churchmanship, the *Hymns* of 1828 seems singularly unworthy."

In 1825/26 Schmucker was also largely responsible for the founding of a synodical seminary at Gettysburg. He taught there, first as sole professor, until 1864. He was a prolific author and had many social concerns in such areas as abolition of slavery, temperance, and women's rights.

His liberal attitude toward other denominations and his qualified acceptance of some of the distinctive tenets of his own church as delineated in the Definite Synodical Platform of 1855 exposed him to much criticism in his later years and he ended his career with less prestige than he had previously enjoyed.

⁸Charles Philip Krauth (1797–1867) was born in New Goshenhoppen, Pa., where his father was teacher and organist at the Lutheran church. He studied medicine in Norfolk, Va., then theology under Dr. D. F. Schaeffer in Frederick, Md. He was licensed as a pastor by the Pennsylvania Ministerium in 1819. His subsequent activities included a pastorate in Virginia, associate editorship of the *Evangelical Lutheran Intelligencer*, and the presidency of the synod of Maryland and Virginia. In 1833 he was called to the seminary at Gettysburg. From 1834 to 1850 he held the position of first president of Pennsylvania College, a classical school founded to furnish suitable students for the

seminary. From 1850 to 1861 he served as the editor of the *Evangelical Review*, a periodical begun by Prof. W. M. Reynolds. In addition to serving on the hymnbook committee he served as the chairman of a committee to prepare an English liturgy in 1841.

9Gottlieb Shober (1756–1838) was a Moravian, born in Bethlehem, Pa., who served as pastor of Lutheran congregations in North Carolina. He was a prominent early member of the North Carolina Synod, one of the founders of the General Synod, and a leader in the dissension which led to the formation of the Tennessee Synod in 1820.

10John George Schmucker (1771–1838) was born in Michaelstadt, Germany and emigrated to America in 1785. At the age of 18 he began the study of theology under his pastor, Rev. Paul Henkel, in Woodstock, Va. In 1790 he moved to Philadelphia to study classics at the University of Pennsylvania and theology under Drs. Helmuth and Schmidt. In 1792 he became a member of the Pennsylvania Ministerium. In 1794 he went to Hagerstown, Md., to serve eight congregations. In 1809 he moved to York, Pa., where he stayed for 26 years. He was "fearless in exposing vice, unfaltering in his advocacy of moral reforms, and warmly attached to the American Bible and Tract Societies." He was instrumental in the founding of the General Synod in 1820 and in 1824 for the formation of the Synod of Western Pennsylvania. He published eight volumes, as well as pamphlets, all but two in German, and left a manuscript of a practical and exegetical commentary on the Epistle to the Hebrews.

11Benjamin Keller was born at Lancaster, Pa., and was educated for the ministry by G. H. E. Muhlenberg (H. M. Muhlenberg's youngest son) there. He served pastorates in Pennsylvania at Carlisle, Germantown, and the "College Church" at Gettysburg. He also founded St. Jacobus (German) church and sustained the missions at Nicetown and Rising Sun, Philadelphia. He was also an agent of the Lutheran Board of Publications in Philadelphia.

121850.

13By mid-19th century developments in Germany were being reflected in America, and there was evidence of a growth in confessional and churchly consciousness. In 1850 the Ministerium of Pennsylvania resolved to seek the cooperation of the synods of New York, Ohio, and the General Synod in the preparation of a revised agenda. A definite effort was made to return to a somewhat greater confessional clarity and a responsive type of service. In the service which this committee prepared, the principal parts of the old Lutheran Liturgy were restored, generally in proper order. Definite reference was made to the Lutheran Confessions and the text of the Augsburg Confession was included. It might be surmised that some of these same influences were beginning to be felt in the area of hymnody in 1845.

14It may be noted that the committee constituted in 1845 was vastly enlarged from the original committee. A wide geographical area is now represented and a proliferation of synods was involved.

15Although no documentation has been found for the "sub-committee of three," it seems possible that the work was delegated to two members of the original hymnal committee (S. S. Schmucker and C. P. Krauth) who were working at Gettysburg. The third member apparently was William M. Reynolds who was also a professor at Gettysburg at the time.

16The numerous additions, deletions, and revisions can be documented upon examination of the hymnals themselves, although casual inspection does not necessarily yield the rationale for many of the changes. Representative titles of hymns omitted in the revised edition are such as "An alien from God and a stranger to grace," "Attracted by love's sacred force," "Death! `tis a melancholy day," and "Vain man, on foolish pleasures bent." Additions to the revised edition include "Almighty God, thy word is cast;" "As the eagle fondly hovers," a translation from Gerhardt; "A safe stronghold our God is still," a translation from Luther; as well as "Ye glitt'ring toys of earth, adieu." The hymns in the revised edition numbered about 1000. A later revision in 1852 contained 1024 hymns.

[17]Hymns translated from the German are relatively few in number. Gerhardt is represented by three and Luther by seven. W. M. Reynolds and a "Dr. Mills" are the main translators referred to, accounting for nine of the above.

[18]The index of subjects begins with "Abhorrence of sin" and ends with "Zion's increase, prayer for." The extreme detail of the index might be illustrated by the following examples:

> Minister, farewell charge of a
>> at ordination of a
>> at installation of a
>> at settlement of a
>> praise upon obtaining a
>> dangerous illness of a
>> death of a
>> funeral of a faithful

[19]William Morton Reynolds (1812–1876) was born in Fayette County, Pa., and was a graduate of both Jefferson College at Canonsburg and the Gettysburg Theological Seminary. He was a professor at Pennsylvania College (affiliated with the seminary) from 1833 to 1850, except for 1835/36 when he served as a pastor at Deerfield, NJ. In 1850 he became president of Capital University at Columbus, O., and subsequently held the same position at Illinois State University from 1857 to 1860. In 1864 he entered the ministry of the Protestant Episcopal Church; according to Jacobs, who personally interviewed Reynolds in later years, his "sole motive in leaving the Church in which he had done distinguished and valuable service was that every door for employment was closed against him."

He was founder of the *Evangelical Review*, translator of a *History of New Sweden* in 1874, and translator of a number of hymns from the German, in addition to serving as an editor for the General Synod's hymnbook in 1850.

[20]Charles Frederick Schaeffer (1807–1879) was a graduate of the University of Pennsylvania who studied theology under his father, Dr. F. D. Schaeffer, and his brother-in-law, Dr. C. R. Demme. He was a pastor at Carlisle, Pa.; Hagerstown, Md.; Lancaster, Ohio; Red Hook, N.Y.; and Easton, Pa. He was professor of theology at Columbus, Ohio, from 1840–1845, at Gettysburg from 1857–1864, and at Philadelphia from 1864 until his death. He was the translator of a book on *Acts* and Kurtz's *Sacred History*; he edited the American edition of Arndt's *True Christianity*; he authored a commentary on *Matthew*; he frequently contributed to the *Evangelical Review*. He was also an influential leader of the movement that resulted in the formation of the General Council in 1867.

10

Evangelische Liedersammlung[1]

genommen aus der Liedersammlung und dem Gemeinschaftlichen Gesangbuch, zum bequemeren Gebrauch in den evangelischen Gemeinen

Gettysburg: Stereotypirt von L. Johnson, 1834[2]

A Collection of Evangelical Hymns

Selected from the Collection of Devotional Hymns and the Common Hymn Book, suitable for use in evangelical congregations

Gettysburg: L. Johnson, 1834

Preface

The editors of this hymnal are warm admirers of the previous hymnbooks of the evangelical churches; but they also know that their concern was not only for public worship, but at the same time also for the edification of the home. On this account the collections have grown to be thick, unhandy volumes which especially the young people in congregations do not purchase nor take with them to church.

The present collection is compiled on the basis of a careful choice from the *Liedersammlung*[3] and the *Gemeinschaftlich Gesangbuch*[4] and is intended to remedy the deficiency that is well known and to facilitate everyone's singing and edification at worship.

Many hymns in the current hymnals have no melodies at all assigned to them, and others are so difficult that they could almost never be sung in the churches. Such hymns we have here omitted, and have added others set to easier melodies, also some to common English melodies.

A number of hymns have 15 to 20 stanzas, so that they are not nearly all sung at worship. In such cases we have, after long deliberation, made a selection of stanzas, thus shortening the hymn, yet in such a way as to retain the continuity of the thought so that a complete subject matter still remains.[5]

Finally, our collections, in the overall view, are still incomplete. We have no mission hymns at all, only a single one for a general revival, none for prayer meetings or services in the home, and for other important religious subjects. This deficiency we have here supplied in an appendix, since God's messages of grace from above demand in our days that such religious sentiments be continually awakened and nourished.

For that reason the General Synod,[6] at the request of numerous brothers and the special conferences of the West and East Pennsylvania Synods, saw fit to prepare such a small, complete hymnal at a low price.[7]

So go forth, then, little volume, and commend yourself to the hearts of all true children of God and to all evangelical congregations which will find you deserving of their love and acceptance.

May He who assigns each grain of sand its place, and who knows how to use each one, use also you for the salvation of souls of His dearly purchased mankind!

N.B. This book can also be used without difficulty where many congregation members still have the old book, if the preacher will choose only hymns that have been borrowed from the old book in use, and if after he announces the number of the hymn in the new book, he will also announce the number in the old book together with the stanzas that shall be sung. The number of the hymn in the old book and the stanza numbers are appended to each hymn.

J. G. Schmucker,[8] D. D., Senior Preacher
of the Ev. Lutheran Congregation in York, Pa.

F. Meyer, Preacher
of the Lutheran Congregation in Somerset, Pa.
A. Lochman,[9] A. M.,
Preacher of the Lutheran Congregation in Harrisburg, Pa.

July 10, 1833

We the undersigned testify that this hymnbook was submitted for publication in accordance with a resolution of the General Synod.

E. L. Hazelius,[10] D. D.
S. S. Schmucker,[11] D. D.

Gettysburg, July 10, 1833

D. F. Schaeffer,[12] A. M.
J. G. Morris,[13] A. M

Notes

[1]This hymnbook contained 360 hymns plus an appendix of 35 additional hymns.

[2]This volume was entered in copyright in 1833 and apparently first appeared in that year, although I have not seen a copy from that year.

[3]Heinrich Melchior Muhlenberg's *Erbauliche Liedersammlung* of 1786.

[4]*Das Gemeinschaftliche Gesangbuch zum gottesdienstlichen Gebrauch der Lutherischen und Reformierten Gemeinden in Nord-Amerika* published in Baltimore in 1817 was the first of several similar volumes intended for use where Lutherans and Reformed shared the same church building, a not uncommon practice at the time. The references in the *Evangelische Liedersammlung* marked "G" clearly refer to the 1817 book.

[5]Nicum in his *Geschichte des New York Ministeriums* (pp. 194–95) indicates that in J. G. Schmucker's indications to the printer concerning which stanzas of a hymn were to be included, the dash as in st. 1–5, was misinterpreted as a comma or as an "und," with the result that only st. 1 and st. 5 were included. This must have been true only for the printing in 1833, for my copy, dated 1834, has corrected this error.

[6]The General Synod of the Evangelical Lutheran Church in the United States of America was formed in 1820 as a federation of several Lutheran Synods (Pennsylvania Ministerium, New York Ministerium, North Carolina Synod, and Synod of Maryland and Virginia). From its beginning the General Synod did not adhere to a strict Lutheran confessionalism, its constitution

mentioning neither the Lutheran Confessions nor the Bible. Yet its existence did prevent many Lutherans from joining the sects and diminished the danger of merging with the Reformed churches in Pennsylvania and in the South. The inclusion of hymns from *Das Gemeinschaftliche Gesangbuch* was apparently a willing concession in that direction, as the inclusion of revival-type hymnody reflected the developing revivalism of the expanding frontier.

[7]The preparation of a new hymnbook was discussed by the General Synod already in 1827, but no action was taken. A few years later, the General Synod proceeded with plans for a new selection of German hymns and appointed a committee of J. G. Schmucker, F. Heyer, A. Lochman, E. L. Hazelius. S. S. Schmucker, D. F. Schaeffer, and J. G. Morris to prepare a new book. By 1833 it was reported that the new book was completed and at the press. (See *Verhandlungen der Gen. Synode der Evangelish–Lutherischen Kirche in den Vereinigten Staaten von Nord-Amerika, 1827, 1833;* also Nicum, *Geschichte des Evangelisch-Lutherischen Ministeriums vom Staate New York und angrenzenden Staaten und Ländern.* Reading, Pa., 1888. p. 193.)

[8]John G. Schmucker (1771–1854) was born in Michaelstadt, Germany, emigrating with his father in 1785. He began his preparation for the ministry under Rev. Paul Henkel and later studied theology with Drs. Helmuth and Schmidt. He became a member of the Pennsylvania Ministerium in 1792 and spent his pastoral ministry in Hagerstown, Md., and York, Pa., and vicinity. He was prominent in the founding of the General Synod and of the theological seminary at Gettysburg, where his son, S. S. Schmucker, served for many years.

[9]Augustus H. Lochman (1802–91) studied theology under his father, whom he succeeded as pastor in Harrisburg, Pa., in 1826. In 1836 he moved to York, Pa., where he was pastor of Christ Church for many years.

[10]Ernest Louis Hazelius (1777–1853) was a prominent educator in the Lutheran church. After teaching in the Moravian school at Nazareth, Pa., he was ordained to the Lutheran ministry by the New York Ministerium in 1809. He taught at Hartwick Seminary, Gettysburg, and Lexington, S. C.

[11]Samuel Simon Schmucker (1799–1873) was probably the "best educated young man, of American birth, in the Lutheran ministry" of his day. He was one of the guiding spirits of the General Synod, the first professor at its seminary in Gettysburg, and chief proponent of the movement of "American Lutheranism."

[12]David Frederick Schaeffer (1787–1837) was one of the founders of the General Synod, which he also served as secretary and later as president. He was editor of *The Lutheran Intelligencer*, the first English Lutheran periodical in America.

[13]John Gottlieb Morris (1803–1895) was a student of S. S. Schmucker and served as pastor in Baltimore, Md., and Lutherville. Md. His father was a distinguished surgeon in the Revolutionary Army.

11

Evangelisch-Lutherisches Kirchengesangbuch[1]

The earliest examples of the return to a more confessional hymnody in America are J. A. A. Grabau's Evangelisch-Lutherisches Kirchengesangbuch (1842) and C. F. W. Walther's Kirchengesangbuch (1847). Grabau was the leader of a group of Prussian emigrants who settled in and near Buffalo, New York; Walther was the leader of a group of Saxon immigrants who settled in Perry County, Missouri, and in St. Louis. Both groups came to America fully committed to a strong confessional position and their hymn books reflect a vigorous and conscious return to the use of the Lutheran chorale heritage.

Evangelisch Lutherisches Kirchengesangbuch

Buffalo: Gedruckt mit Georg Zahm's Schriften, 1842

Evangelical Lutheran Church Hymnbook

Buffalo: Printed at Georg Zahm's Press, 1842

I(n) (the) N(ame) (of) J(esus)

Foreword

This Christian Hymnbook is presented in its present form because of the urgent requirements of several Lutheran congregations, and in the compilation the following old hymnbooks have been used: (1) Luther's Hymnbook, augmented with a second part, Leipzig, 1559 and 1561;[2] (2) that of Pomerania; (3) that of Thuringia; (4) that of Dresden; (5) that of Gotha; (6) that of Weimar; (7) that of Schwarzburg (Arnstadt); (8) that of Schwarzburg (Rudolfstadt); (9) that of Hamburg; (10) that of Magdeburg; (11 that of Brandenburg; (12) the Lower-Saxon *Liederkern* (Hildesheim); (13) that of Altenburg; (14) that of Braunschweig; (15) that of Hanover; (16) that of Waldeck; (17) that of Marburg; (18) that of Halle (on the Saale); (19) that of Steinmetz (Cloister Bergen); (20) the *Porst* (Berlin); (21) that of Breslau; (22) that of Stade (Hanover); (23) The Hymns of Paul Gerhardt (Unaltered, Wittenberg, 1723); (24) two old Lutheran hymnbooks without a title, printed around 1700; (25) that of Stollberg; (26) that of Altona; (27) that of Naumburg; (28) several old Lutheran prayer books with hymns; further: (29) The Saxon Electoral Order of Worship of 1580; (30) The Coburg-Saxon Order of Worship of 1626; (31) an order of worship of 1571 (Austria below Enns); (32) the Pomeranian Order of Worship of 1563 and 1690; (33) the Herzog-Heinrich church agenda of 1536.

The book follows the needs of the people who have demanded it and is at the same time, in our opinion, a testimony that we in our church services will espouse nothing peculiar but will follow in the footsteps of our believing forefathers and the entire pure Lutheran Church, as is proper according to God's Word, Hebrews 13:7: "Remember them which have the rule over you, who have spoken unto you the Word of God: whose faith follow, considering the end of their conversation."

To insure reliable consistency of the hymn text, the original version has, wherever possible, been maintained throughout.

The General Prayers contain those petitions, intercessions, prayers of praise and thanksgiving (as many old hymnbooks and prayer-books testify) on which the church has agreed. The Prefaces, Collects, and Rubrics of the Christian order of worship have been taken from the aforementioned agendas and orders of worship. They are placed, as in Luther's hymnbook, not in the back as an appendix, but by themselves in each section.

The order and sequence of the hymn sections, of which there are 40, follow the old pattern, which is: I. the entire church year, and II. the entire contents of Luther's Small Catechism. The first 19 sections embrace the course of the church year, and from section 20 on, the contents of the Catechism.

Concerning the retention of the pure, old Latin hymns, Dr. Luther says in his hymnbook at No. 52: *Dies est laetitiae* (The Day Is Joyful): "We also have included these old hymns as a testimony of those devout Christians who lived before us in the darkness of false doctrine. So that one can easily see that at all times there were those who knew Christ aright and were marvelously kept in this same knowledge through God's grace."

The modest size of the book, which already has become larger than originally planned, could embrace only that which properly belongs in the worship service of the church. As God further bestows His grace through Jesus Christ, we hope that a special little book can be made, which would contain the Gospels and Epistles, the Passion History of Christ, Morning and Evening Devotions, Confessional and Communion Devotions, and other things that would make it complete. This could then be bound together with this hymnbook.

In the present hymnbook none of the hymns have been abbreviated because of great length except two or three, where it seemed really advisable because of length and copiousness. In most of the older hymnbooks much more has been abbreviated; this we have not wanted to imitate. We wanted to avoid the appearance of prejudice against hymnbooks that are not abbreviated; on the contrary, we wanted to promote unity.

In order to save space, several doxologies which can be added to many hymns are presented as separate hymns with their own numbers. For example, "Ehr sei Gott Vater allezeit." They can be used more easily and more frequently in this way as special little hymns, as the opportunity presents itself.

May the merciful God, who has done great things for us, for the sake of Jesus Christ, His Son, bless this work begun and completed with His gracious help, to the praise of His name and for the salvation of our beloved congregations and many other dearly redeemed souls. To Him be honor now and in eternity. Amen.

Buffalo, the 10th of December, 1842

The Publisher: Johann Andreas August Grabau,
Lutheran pastor

The Hymnbook Commission
of the Lutheran congregation at Buffalo
J. A. A. Grabau,[3]
E. Krieg,
W. Hachemann.

The Congregational Elders
Ernst Krieg,
Friedrich Luetke,
Rudolph Krause,
Gottfried Schoenfeld,
Christian Rother,
Johann Heuer

Notes

[1]This hymnal was produced by Rev. J. A. A. Grabau (1804–79) for the use of a number of congregations of Prussian immigrants who arrived in America in 1839 and settled at Buffalo, New York and Milwaukee, Wisconsin. While originally the product of a single congregation, with the formation of the Buffalo Synod in 1845, Grabau's hymnbook was officially adopted by the synod and introduced into all its congregations. The first edition contained 491 hymns.

[2]This later reprint of Valentin Babst's hymnal of 1545 was the last hymnal for which Luther had written a preface and was probably the most representative Lutheran hymnbook of its time. Grabau's use of the Babst hymnal is clearly shown in that he follows its arrangement in placing prayers, collects, and other liturgical material throughout the book with the particular season of the church year to which they pertain, rather than in an appendix at the end of the book. Over half of the hymns in the Babst hymnbook are included in Grabau's book, including some of the Latin hymns which were printed in Latin.

[3]Johannes Andreas August Grabau (1804–79) was a pastor at Erfurt, Germany, who resisted the imposition of a uniform liturgy which he considered Reformed in character, an act for which he was twice imprisoned. Eventually he emigrated to America with members of congregations from Erfurt, Magdeburg, and elsewhere, arriving in America in the early days of 1839. The Prussian emigrants under Grabau were a strictly confessional group, and for a short tine the possibility existed that this stance would help unite the Prussians, the Saxons, and the emissaries of Wilhelm Loehe in Michigan and Indiana. However differing views of the church and the ministry provoked a controversy between the Missouri Synod and the Buffalo Synod, which prevented any further united efforts.

12

Kirchengesangbuch für Evangelisch-Lutherische Gemeinden ungeänderter Augsburgischer Confession

darin des seligen D. Martin Luthers und anderer geistreichen Lehrer gebraeuchlichste Kirchen-Lieder enthalten sind.

New York: Gedruckt für die Herausgeber bei H. Ludwig. Im Verlag der deutschen evang. luth. Gemeinde u. A. C. in St. Louis, Mo., 1847

Church Hymnbook for Evangelical Lutheran Congregations of the Unaltered Augsburg Confession

Containing the most useful church hymns of the Blessed Dr. Martin Luther and other spiritual teachers.

New York: Printed for the publisher by H. Ludwig. Published by the German Evangelical Lutheran Congregation of the Augsburg Confession in St. Louis, Mo., 1847

[This publication contained no preface or introductory material. An unsigned article in Der Lutheraner,[1] *however, describes the book at the time of its appearance. It is probable that C. F. W. Walther himself wrote the article which is given below.]*

The new "Hymnal for Evangelical Lutheran Congregations of the Unaltered Augsburg Confession," announced in number 12 of this publication, edited by several Lutheran pastors in Missouri and published by the local Lutheran congregation,[2] has now left the press. Its layout is as follows: pages I–XII contain in addition to the title, the table of contents and an alphabetical list of the hymns; pages 1–380 contain the hymns, 437 in all; pages 381–390 contain the index to the tunes; and pages 391–420 the *first appendix*, consisting of morning, evening, confessional, Communion, sick, deathbed, and other prayers, the formula for an emergency baptism, the usual antiphons, and so forth. The Small Catechism of Luther constitutes a *second appendix*, and the three ecumenical creeds and the Unaltered Augsburg Confession, a *third* [appendix]. The entire volume consists of 516 pages in the usual format of a German hymnal, with the type of the new New York edition of Luther's *Hauspostille*.

The price per copy, well bound in leather, pressed, with marbled edges, is 75 cents. Mr. Ludwig of New York was kind enough to arrange for the printing and binding; consequently there is no need for the assurance that the outward makeup of the book will certainly be satisfactory to all who use it.

In the selection of the adopted hymns the chief consideration was that they be pure in doctrine; that they have found almost universal acceptance within the orthodox German Lutheran Church and have thus received the almost unanimous testimony that they had come forth from the true spirit (of Lutheranism); that they express not so much the changing circumstances of individual persons but rather contain the language of the whole church, because the book is to be used primarily in public worship; and finally that they, though bearing the imprint of Christian simplicity, be not merely rhymed prose but the creations of a truly Christian poetry.

The editors have been fully conscious of the difficulty of their task; they have altogether despaired of their own wisdom and pleaded earnestly with God for the illumination and direction of His Holy Spirit and especially for the gift of trying and discerning the spirits. They can give the assurance that they approached the task with fear and trembling and from the Christian church's voluminous treasury of German hymnody, according to the grace which God has given them, selected only those hymns which they recognized as particularly worthy of transmission from children to children's children and of preservation as a treasure, as an inalienable possession of the German-speaking church. May our Lord Jesus Christ, who ascended on high and gave gifts to men, grant a superabundant blessing also on this little hymnal.

With this hymnal for the church the needs of the home were indeed not overlooked, even though, as said, the primary purpose was to serve the church. So we have thought that we might in time also follow this up with a special hymnal for the home as part two, if the demand for it becomes clear in the congregations.[3]

Because the editors felt it essential to give the most valuable hymns in so small a hymnal, only little thought could be given to a general acquaintance with their appropriate melodies.

However, the index to the tunes in most cases refers to better-known melodies for substitution where the suggested tune is not too well known. In addition we are also considering the publication of a lithographed book of melodies within the next several months as a companion to our hymnal[4] in order to relieve a possible difficulty in some of our parishes. We are also of the opinion that we have great cause to be concerned about the proper preservation of the wonderful, rich treasury of our church melodies.[5]

Notes

[1](C. F. W. Walther). "Lutherisches Kirchen-Gesangbuch," *Der Lutheraner*, III (15 June, 1847), 84. The translation is from Carl S. Meyer, ed., *Moving Frontiers: Readings in the History of the Lutheran Church—Missouri Synod*, Concordia Publishing House, 1964, 163–64. Reproduced with permission.

[2]In November, 1845, C. F. W. Walther brought to the attention of the Gesamtgemeinde ("federated congregation") of St. Louis, of which he was the pastor, the need for a new hymnal. On November 17, 1845, the congregation resolved to proceed with plans for a new hymnal. While this notice indicates the involvement of "several Lutheran pastors in Missouri," undoubtedly Walther himself took the leading role. The new book was apparently

introduced for the first time in the St. Louis Gesamtgemeinde on Sunday, August 15, 1847. The following October the congregation resolved to give Walther "five cords of winter wood together with a week's salary in appreciation for his labors in connection with the hymnbook." See Carl Schalk, *The Roots of Hymnody in the Lutheran Church—Missouri Synod*, Concordia Publishing House, 1965.

[3]This possibility was apparently never realized.

[4]Advertisements in *Der Lutheraner* in 1851 refer to just such a melody book, a collection of *Melodien deutscher Kirchengesaenge nach Dr. Friedrich Layriz*. Other references in 1852 and the appearance in 1857 of *223 Melodien deutscher Kirchengesaenge* are apparently adaptations of similar books of Layriz published in Germany in 1839, 1848, and 1850.

[5]From its earliest beginnings The Lutheran Church—Missouri Synod vigorously promoted the use of the rhythmic form of the chorale melodies. Between 1847 and 1854 the pages of *Der Lutheraner* carried four major articles extolling the virtues of the rhythmic chorale; by 1849 the St. Louis congregation held regular practice sessions for the purpose of learning the melodies; and the use of various editions of Layriz *Kern des deutschen Kirchengesangs* and later the publication of their own various chorale books served to continue the support of the rhythmic chorale.

13

Choralbuch mit Liturgie und Chorgesängen zum Kirchenbuch der Allgemeinen Kirchenversammlung

Three important chorale books that provided organ settings to support the more confessional hymn books which sought to restore the Lutheran chorale were: Endlich's Choralbuch *(1879), a companion volume for the General Council's* Kirchenbuch *(1877); and Hoelter's* Choralbuch *(1886) and Brauer's* Mehrstimmiges Choralbuch *(1888), both of which supported Walther's* Kirchengesangbuch *(1847).*

Each of these books reflects the growing interest in the recovery of the rhythmic form of the chorale for the purpose of reinvigorating congregational singing which—as a result of the erosions of rationalism and Pietism—had become dreary, lugubrious, drab, and dull.

Choralbuch mit Liturgie
und Chorgesängen zum Kirchenbuch
der Allgemeinen
Kirchenversammlung

Bearbeitet von J. Endlich.[1] Philadelphia: The
United Lutheran Publication House, 1879

Chorale Book with Liturgy and Choir Anthems for the Church Book of the General Council

CHORALBUCH MIT LITURGIE UND CHORGESÄNGEN

Compiled by J. Endlich. Philadelphia: The United
Lutheran Publication House, 1879

Because of the importance of the liturgical portion and the
larger number of proper melodies that have been incorporated
in the hymnal of the General Council,[2] the undersigned (as a
musician member of the committee) has been authorized by the
hymnological committee of the Council to review these portions
of the hymnal. This laborious and expensive task was
undertaken without any thought of remuneration or honor, but
out of an inner desire to restore to the church also the musical
settings that have been lacking in the past, as the Church-book[3]
has already accomplished in hymn and word. In Germany much
laudable work has been done in this respect compared with the
little work done here in America. Without the motivation of the
Church-book, we would have to wait even longer to recapture
the stately old chorales and liturgical settings.

A work such as this presents many difficulties here (in
America) because of the sketchy nature of the original sources.
To acquire the necessary works from Germany would have been
very costly and unreliable. So, for example, the works of
Lossius, so indispensable for the liturgical section, was not
promptly forthcoming in spite of repeated orders to Germany.

The desires and wishes of experienced organists and choir
directors were gladly complied with, and they accordingly were
decisive for the basic principles of the work, namely, settings
for mixed choir which would also serve as convenient
accompaniments for congregational singing.

The complete work has two parts:
  (1) The liturgical settings, with supplementary choir
     settings
  (2) The chorales

The main sources used for the liturgical music were:
  Spangenberg, *Kirchengesänge*, 1545
  Wolfgang, Pfalzgrafen bei Rhein, *Kirchenordnung*, 1570
  Pommerische Kirchenordnung, 1563
  Schoeberlein, *Schatz des liturgischen Chor- und Gemeinde-
     gesangs*, 1865
  Lorzing, *Psalter*, 1876, and other old and new works.

An oversight that cannot be remedied immediately is the fact that the individual pieces of the liturgical section were not always accompanied by their original sources. Schoeberlein was used frequently here, and a number of older items revised according to the original. It cannot be disapproved that the psalm tone antiphons in the Vesper service were transposed to the key of A, since it brings them within comfortable pitch for easier congregational singing and will through repeated use provide greater security. Where possible, bar lines were introduced, because this makes learning the pieces and overall use easier. Dr. Spaeth[4], in another publication, has made the necessary explanations for the use of the various liturgical parts. In addition to the above-mentioned sources, the following were consulted regarding the chorales:

Wolfgang, Ammon, *Neues Gesangbuch*, 1591
Dresdner Gesangbuch, 1622
Rist, *Himmlische Lieder*, 1652 (mit Schops *Choraelen*)
Joh. Crueger, *Praxis pietatis melica*, 1666
Koenig's *Harmonischer Liederschatz*, 1738
Knecht, *Choralbuch*, 1799
Winterfeld, *Evangelischer Kirchengesang*, 1843
Wuertemberg'sches Choralbuch, 1844
Tucher, *Melodieen des evang. Kirchengesangs*, 1848
Layriz, *Kern des deutschen Kirchengesangs*, 1854
Die Melodieen des deutschen evang. Kirchengesangbuchs,
    Tucher, Faiszt, and Zahn, 1854
Kocher, *Zionsharfe*, 1855
Ritter, *Choralbuch*, 1856
Zahn, *Vierstimmiges Melodienbuch*, 1868
Hommel, *Geistliche Volkslieder*, 1871
Ihme, *Hallelujah*, 1875

Musical settings of Michael Praetorius, Schein, and other old masters sometimes had to suffer transpositions and other minor alterations in the lower and inner voices in order to abide by the basic principles of this work. This was done with great reluctance. The changes were made, however, so as not to alter the spirit of the original. Only the year in which the melody first appeared is ordinarily given in the case of these chorales. It would have been in order also to indicate "setting by Praetorius" or "Schein" and the date of the setting. The newer chorales, those from the end of the 17th century on, are retained in their dependable original settings whenever possible; the rest were freely harmonized. Included are several melodies from the Bohemian Brethren and a few from Hommel's *Geistliche Volkslieder*, which should prove to be a welcome addition. A great deal of time was spent on research and comparison of the melodies, so that they might be accepted and looked upon as genuine and pure.

A goodly number of the chorales also have English translations in addition to the German text. Though the chorale has gained a place in the *Churchbook* by Miss Krauth—which is considered official by the English Lutheran churches—it has not as yet established itself in this church. This is deeply regretted by many who know how much loss there has been in the church service on this account. For if the choirs in the English churches would get used to singing a chorale occasionally, the hearts and minds of English Lutheran congregations would soon be open to them, and the glorious rhythmic chorale would find a home there, as it should.

Finally, the choir numbers, with the exception of a few melodies of the Bohemian Brethren from Zahn (*Geistliche Lieder der Brüder in Boehmen und Maehren*), have been taken from Schoeberlein. They are above the average ability of our church choirs, but it is hoped that they will not be entirely neglected and that they may serve to check the present trend toward exceedingly dull choir music in our churches that is often unfitting for the church. This is one of the main reasons for including these choir selections here.

Several fellow members of the committee were of great assistance in this endeavor through kind loans of valuable works of the old masters. Dr. Spaeth must be credited with active participation in the project from beginning to end, for without his help and advice insurmountable problems would have arisen.

May the Lord not withhold His blessing from this work, which is freely offered to be of service to the church. May He open new doors for this book so that the treasures offered in it may again become the common treasure of our church, which is singularly blessed also in song. God grant it:

J. Endlich

Notes

[1]Resources available to the editor have failed to disclose any significant biographical information regarding the compiler of this chorale book.

[2]*Kirchenbuch für Evangelisch-Lutherische Gemeinden*. Herausgegeben von der Allgemeinen Versammlung der Evangelishe-Lutherischen Kirche in Nord-Amerika (Philadelphia: General Council Publication Board, 1877).

[3]The *Church Book for the Use of Evangelical Lutheran Congregations*, published in 1868 by the General Council, had been provided with a music edition prepared by Harriet Reynolds Krauth and published seven years earlier in 1872. Endlich's task was to provide a similar resource for the *Kirchenbuch*, the German hymnbook of the General Council.

[4]Dr. Adolph Spaeth was a member of the committee appointed at the first convention of the General Council in 1867 in Ft. Wayne, Indiana to prepare the *Kirchenbuch*.

14

Choralbuch[1]

Eine Sammlung der gangbarsten Choräle der evang.-lutherischen Kirche, meist nach Dr. Layriz,[2] nebst den wichtigsten liturgischen Sätzen

St. Louis, Mo. Concordia Publishing House, 1886

Chorale Book

A collection of the most useful chorales of the Evangelical Lutheran Church, taken primarily from Dr. Fr. Layriz, together with the most important liturgical settings.

St. Louis, Mo. Concordia Publishing House, 1886

Preface

The publication of a new book should always be justified by its need. What is the case with this chorale book?

Our synod is a pioneer also with regard to the cultivation of rhythmic congregational song,[3] however, until now it has not provided for a chorale book. At first it was not necessary because one could obtain the second edition of Layriz "Kern."[4] When this edition was out of print and the third edition appeared with changes in the melodies and settings, it was almost considered a forgery, and people were very happy when a private individual undertook to reprint a portion of the chorales from the second edition.[5] However, people soon perceived that Layriz had been correct in changing in part the melodies and settings of this third edition by going back to the original version. Further, one could hardly forever shut one's eyes to the research and work of Herzog,[6] Zahn,[7] and others, just as little as the work of restoring the songs of our hymnbook to their original and unfalsified version could be omitted. Moreover, the latter contains a number of songs which have very beautiful melodies that were nowhere available to us.

Already a decade ago I[8] sought out the original melodies which are missing from our melody book. Since, however, without the publication of a complete chorale book the introduction of these melodies was not easily possible, and since out of a concern for Christian charity the publication of such a book could not yet be undertaken, the printing of the melodies too was postponed. In the course of time, however, more and more voices were raised that the synod should concern itself to provide for congregational singing, just as it concerns itself with the other needs of congregations through publication of textbooks, devotional material, and school books. Now it so happened that a collection of organ interludes came into the possession of Concordia Publishing House and my assignment was to complete it and prepare it for publication. So the plan matured to publish a chorale book with interludes, cadences, and modulations.[9] It was soon discovered, however, that such a project, if it were to be complete, would be too extensive for Sundays as well as for use in the family, and it was resolved to begin with only the publication of a chorale book, the interludes, etc. to follow later.

Since until now the second edition of Layriz found preferential use among us, I undertook to reproduce it unchanged where it did not contain obvious mistakes contrary to the current practice of harmonization; only the melodies should, wherever possible, be restored to their original form. But while the manuscript was at the printer and many pages had already been electrotyped, the information came to us that Herman Ilse,[10] a teacher in Brooklyn, had also prepared a chorale book. Because I believed that two chorale books would not only be too many, but would be mutually detrimental, I immediately got in touch with him. As a consequence Mr. Ilse came to St. Louis and, in part with the help of Cantor J. G. Kunz,[11] we compared both manuscripts. After that I reworked my manuscript and fashioned the one before you, comparing Layriz with Herzog,

Zahn, Enckhausen,[12] and the old masters. So from both manuscripts has appeared a new one. Where Mr. Ilse and I could not agree, the matter was presented to Mr. Kunz, and we abided by his decision. Only then did I furnish an original when no four-part setting was available.[13]

In connection with the editing of the melodies, we always returned to the original form if it could be located and if the performance of it did not present too great a difficulty. Where it was feared that a certain version was already here to stay, either this form or the original was given as a variant.[14] If the changes are only concerned with the rhythm, this is usually indicated by the use of small notes above the system. Many instances of syncopation have been altered—following Herzog and Zahn—in order to make them more practical. Where a good authority could be found, a quarter note was occasionally changed to a half note, or, vice versa, a half note changed to a quarter note, thereby placing an accented syllable on the strong beat. Although originally I had in mind to include the original melodies for all the chorales in our hymnbook, I soon had to give this up, in part because with some chorales there is a veritable disorder of melodies so that it was impossible to know which melody had become the more accepted, in part because many were too unchurchly or were in the style of arias. I am sorry to say that for the sake of certain hymns several of these melodies had to be included which I would otherwise have rejected.

In order that this chorale book might serve first of all the unison congregational singing, I have had—so far as is practical—the congregation in mind. Some melodies have been set lower in pitch, others higher in pitch than they are in Layriz second edition. The level of pitch, however, was always so chosen that it would be possible for all kinds of voices to sing the melody without great exertion, as far as the compass of the melody permitted.[15]

A completely faithful restoration of the settings of the old masters could not have been part of my purpose. Before Osiander[16] (1586), settings were fashioned only for choirs, and indeed for the most part so sophisticatedly—in part five-voice settings with the cantus firmus in the tenor—that the setting is entirely unsuited for accompanying the congregational singing, because it offers it no solid support. But the organ settings from Osiander to the beginning of our century were prepared for other, less adequate (complete) organs than ours are, or at least might be. The character of these harmonizations reflect a "gloomy austerity and harshness." Layriz also sensed this*

> *"To offset this, I endeavored to follow the rules of the old settings faithfully, but without directly transferring also into our time the gloomy sterness and even harshness of the harmonic system found in the old masters." Layriz, Kern, 1854, Preface.

and here and there sought to improve upon them. How often, however, he resorted to the use of the weak and unchurchly seventh chord in strong, triumphant chorales! This I have diligently avoided. Also in the use of the third have I departed from Layriz and followed Herzog, Zahn, and Enckhausen. I have begun each chorale with a full triad, and in each key which has a minor character I have also concluded with a minor third unless the models named above called for a major third. I was the better able to do this since earlier in our *Schulblatt***

> **Jahr. II, 5. 27. [The article by Karl Brauer, a review of J. G. Kunz's "Vor- und Zwischenspiele zu den gangbarsten Choralmelodien aus 'Kern des deutschen Kirchengesangs von Dr. Fr. Layriz'" published in St. Louis by A. Wiebusch and Son, appeared in the Evang.-Luth. Schulblatt II (Sept. 1866), 26–29, and concluded in II (Oct. 1866), 50–54.]

the rule was given that the third must not be omitted.

Regarding whether or not the major or minor third should be used, I find in "Euterpe"[17] the following: "In the old music in the Dorian, Phrygian, and Aeolian modes the major third is not permitted in the final chord on the tonic." Because it was the opinion of composers that the minor third does not effect a complete conclusion, therefore they omitted the third at the final chord. That they then use the major third in place of the minor third may well lie in the poor temperament of their organs, in which many minor thirds were very impure. Fuchs writes in his Gradus ad parnassum of a special case: "Since the tonality is Dorian, which has a minor third to which the ear has become accustomed throughout the entire chorale, it would be ill suited if at the conclusion the third would be raised; for that reason it would be better if the third were omitted altogether." But with the currently used temperament we have no misgivings about concluding each piece in minor with the minor third. It is reprehensible when one line of a chorale closes in major and the following line must begin again in minor.

I have taken great pains to preserve the peculiarities of the old church modes, which simply cannot be treated on the basis of our modern major-minor system, and which the organist cannot be permitted to cavalierly ignore. This included the almost exclusive use of root position chords together with their first inversion, excluding, as often as possible, especially the seventh chord and the second inversion; it included the use of chord progressions identifying the respective mode and also the avoidance, as much as possible, of chromatic alterations. "Whoever equalizes the rhythm of the melodies and introduces harmonies of our present harmonic system has robbed these works of their essence, and the rugged melodies have become a mere shadow of their former selves.***

***Jacob and Richter, Reformatorisches Choralbuch, Preface.

A few words more concerning the external format of this chorale book.

The fermatas at the end of each line of the chorale have only the purpose of showing the end of the line. Originally the chorales had neither fermatas, bar lines, nor fixed rests, but only certain signs (the so-called caesura mark) to indicate the rhythmic segments. Since, however, at a later time the measure bars were used in order to bring the chorale into conformity with modern principles, therefore the concluding note occasionally had to be lengthened and rests inserted, and the fermata was used to mark pauses in the rhythm. These fermatas therefore do not demand arbitrary prolongation of the respective notes; the chorale is rather to be sung from beginning to end in strict time. If a congregation cannot be trained to sing without pauses where none are to be found, then the organist must be careful that the first note of the following phrase falls on the proper beat.****

****Instructive advice about this matter is contained in the excellent booklet: Jahn, *Handbüchlein für evangelische Kantoren und Organisten*. Bertelsmann, Guetersloh. It can be obtained fromn Concordia Publishing House. Cost, $.90.

In order to avoid inconvenient page turning, it was often necessary to depart from the alphabetical order in the arrangement of the chorales. However, in order to facilitate looking up an item, three indexes are added. The first contains the melodies of the chorales in alphabetical order, as well as the number of the corresponding melodies and the hymn number of all the hymns to be sung according to a given melody. In another index all melodies are arranged according to the poetic meter.

The third index gives the beginning of all the hymns in the St.Louis[19] and Wisconsin hymn books,[20] the Treasury of Prayer,[21] and the Lenten and Easter books,[22] together with the number of the respective melody plus the number in the metrical index. To save room, no text is printed with the notes. There would be little reason to underlay only one stanza of the text, and the printing of the entire hymn does not belong in a chorale book.

Above each chorale a short historical notice has been added which gives either the composer of the melody or its first publisher or, when neither of these is known, the collection in which the chorale first appeared or only the year in which it became a part of the congregational song.

The second section of this chorale book contains mostly chorales which have been included out of consideration for the hymnbook of the Wisconsin Synod, plus the Litany, the Te Deum, and several liturgical settings. With regard to the use of the organ in the liturgy, it should be mentioned that the Preface should always be sung without organ accompaniment. In the remaining parts the organ should accompany only those parts under which chords have been placed

Those works which were used most frequently in the preparation of this chorale book are:

1. Dr. F. Layriz, *Kern des deutschen Kirchengesangs*, 1844 (200 items)
2. Dr. F. Layriz, *Kern des deutschen Kirchengesangs*, 1849 (347 items)
3. Dr. F. Layriz, *Kern des deutschen Kirchengesangs*, 1854 and 1855 (613 items)
4. F. A. L. Jakob and E. Richter, *Reformatorisches Choralbuch* (1337 items)
5. J. Zahn, *Vierstimmiges Melodienbuch*, 1860 (191 items)
6. J. Zahn, *Psalter und Harfe*, 1886 (532 items)
7. J. G. Herzog, *Die Choraele der evangelischen Kirche*
8. J. G. Herzog, *Evangelisches Choralbuch*, 1886 (222 items)
9. G. F. H. Enckhausen, *Hermannsburger Missions-Chor-albuch* 1876 (712 items)
10. *Geist- und Lehrreiches Kirchen- und Haus-Buch*, 1706 (735 items)
11. G. Freiherr von Tucher, *Schatz des evangelischen Kirchengesanges*, Zweiter Theil, 1848 (469 items)
12. J. A. Freylinghausen, *Geistreiches Gesang-Buch*, 1706 (758 items)
13. *Geistliche Lieder*, Leipzig, 1547, Val. Babst (169 items)

14. *Ein uraltes Gesangbuch* (303 items)
15. *Choralbuch,* in Verbindung mit J. Zahn, G. Herzog u. P. Gull bearbeitet von W. Ortloph, 1844 (80 items)
16. *Liturgie lutherischer Gemeindegottesdienste,* (F.Hommel), 1851
17. B. Koenig, *Harmonischer Liederschatz,* 1738 (1900 items)
18. F. Mergner, *Choralbuch,* 1883 (304 items)
19. J. Endlich, *Choralbuch,* 1879 (236 items)
20. *Choralbuch,* von J. G. Bretschneider, Manuscript von 1780

I am sorry to say that I could not get ahold of Schöberlein[23] and Winterfeld,[24] but in doubtful cases I have settled the matter by consulting with Pastor F. Lochner[25] and teacher H. Ilse. Works in isometric rhythm (for example, Lohmeyer, Lehmann, Kuehnau, etc.) were certainly at hand, but understandably could not be used.

In conclusion I shout a hearty "May God reward you!" to all who submitted melodies, loaned books, or in any other way have given a helping hand, of which I should mention especially Dr. C. F. W. Walther,[26] Pastor F. Lochner, and teacher J. G. Kunz, who above all others have lent an active hand to this work.[27] Without their cooperation and encouragement I would scarcely have undertaken the preparation of this chorale book.

May this book then do in its modest way that for which it is intended. May it with the aid of the Holy Ghost serve Christ and His church to the glory of God the Father.

St. Louis, Mo. May 1886
H. F. Hoelter

Notes

[1]The announcement and review of this *Choralbuch* appeared in *Der Lutheraner,* XLII (April 15, 1886), 64, and XLII (July 1, 1886), 104, respectively. Both were signed simply W., presumably C. F. W. Walther. An English translation of the announcement and review (which includes some excerpts from Hoelter's Preface) can be found in A. C. Stellhorn, *Schools of The Lutheran Church—Missouri Synod* (Concordia: St. Louis. 1963), 206-209.

[2]Friedrich Layriz (1808–859), through his various publications, was one of the most influential forces shaping the music of American Lutheranism in the last half of the 19th century. His various Melodienbuecher, his *Kern des deutschen Kirchengesangs,* (1844–55), and the musical settings he provided for

the second edition of Wilhelm Loehe's *Agende* exercised great influence. A German pastor who had studied at Erlangen and Leipzig, Layriz served parishes at Hirschlach, Bayreuth, and Schwanigen.

3See Schalk, Carl. *The Roots of Hymnody in The Lutheran Church—Missouri Synod* (St. Louis: Concordia Publishing House, 1965), pp. 772–73 for the concern of this church body in the promotion of the rhythmic chorale.

4The second edition of F. Layriz's "Kern" was published in 1849. The first edition appeared in 1844.

5This publication was undertaken by Mr. L. Volkening, a private St. Louis publisher and appeared in 1863 as the *Evangelish-Lutherisches Choralbuch für Kirche und Haus*. Later editions appeared in 1871, 1874, 1879, and 1883.

6See Nos. 7 and 8 in this list of resources named by Hoelter at the conclusion of this Preface.

7See Nos. 5 and 6 in the list of resources at the conclusion of the Preface. Zahn's monumental *Die Melodien der deutschen evangelischen Kirchenlieder* was not published until 1888–93.

8Heinrich F. Hoelter (1846–1916). Born in Cleveland, Ohio, Hoelter attended the teachers college in Fort Wayne, Ind. He served in Washington, D.C., St. Louis, Mo. (Zion Lutheran Church), and Pittsburgh, Pa., returning to St. Louis where he served Holy Cross Lutheran Church until his death. He was active in both educational and musical circles, was a friend of President Abraham Lincoln and had frequent contact with him. His chief musical efforts were this *Choralbuch* and a collection of interludes for organ. (*Ev. luth. Schulblatt* LI (March, 1916), 86–87.

9*Mit Zwischenspielen, Tonschluessen und Ueberleitungen.*

10Ludwig Herman Ilse (1845–1931) was born in Hanover, Germany. Educated at Concordia Teachers College, Addison, Ill., he served as teacher and organist successively at Pittsburgh. Pa. (First Trinity); Chicago, Ill. (Zion); Brooklyn, N.Y. (St. John's, and later Trinity); and in Bedford, Ohio (Zion), as organist. His publications includes *Chorbuch* (with Wm. Burhenn); *Taschenchorbuch* (with Wm. Burhenn); *Zwischenspiele; Saengerfreund; Kantional für Maennerchor*; this *Choralbuch* (with H. F. Hoelter); and later, together with H. A. Polack, he served as music editor of the *Evangelical Lutheran Hymn-book* (1912).

11 J. G. Kunz (1824–89) was a teacher at Immanuel Lutheran School in St. Louis from 1863 until his death. Born in Germany (Tringenstein), he came to Fort Wayne. Ind., in 1853, where he also served as teacher and organist. Kunz wrote preludes and postludes, *Choraele für Maennerchor, Liederbuch für Oberklassen*, Immanuel's *Saengerbund*, and assisted D. Meibohm in the editing of Meibohm's *Vorspielbuch* (*Ev. Luth. Schulblatt*, XXV (Jan. 1890), 10–15.)

12See item 9 in the list of musical resources at the conclusion of the Preface.

13There is nothing to indicate which are Hoelter's original settings; however, No. 30 is indicated as J. G. Kunz's harmonization, while Nos. 199 and 325 are apparently original tunes by Kunz

14There are seven examples: Nos. 26, 129, 176, 208, 254, 288, 296.

15It is clear that nothing other than unison congregational singing was envisioned by Hoelter.

16Lucas Osiander (1534–1604). Osiander's *Fünfzig Geistliche Lieder und Psalmen* (1586) is usually referred to as the beginning of the general acceptance of the simple "cantional style"—simple homorhythmic choral settings in four or five parts, melody in the soprano part—which ultimately led to the accompaniment of the congregational singing by the organ.

17The origin of this quotation has not been found.

18The depths to which congregational singing had fallen in Germany in the 19th century—a condition which was reflected also in America—is aptly described in a passage from the *Evang. Kirchen-Zeitung*, 1847, No. 84: "Each syllable is sung without distinction for a period of about four beats; on the last syllable of each line or at the end of the melodic phrase there follows a long fermata lasting 8–12 beats, the last part of which is incorporated in a more or less intricate organ interlude. So all the melodies follow one line after the other in this repetitious manner, whether sad or joyous, mournful or exultant, all performed in a creeping, dragging fashion." It is to counteract such a practice that Hoelter's suggestion is made.

19The *Kirchengesangbuch für Evangelisch–Lutherische Gemeinden ungeaenderter Augsburgischer Confession* was published in 1847. It was largely the work of C. F. W. Walther and became an official hymnbook of the Missouri Synod.

20*Evang.-Lutherisches Gesangbuch fur Kirche, Schule und Haus.*

21*Evangelish-Lutherischer Gebets-Schatz;* vollständige Sammlung von Gebeten Dr. Martin Luthers u. a. . . . . Nebst einem Hausgesangbüchlein (St. Louis: Concordia Publishing House.)

22Lochner, Friedrich. *Passionsbuch; Andachten zur häuslichen Feier der heiligen Passionszeit* (St. Louis: M. C. Barthel, 1877); and Lochner, Friedrich. *Osterbuch: Andachten zur häuslichen Feier der heiligen Osterzeit* (St. Louis: Lutherischer Concordia Verlag, 1879).

23Schöberlein, Ludwig. *Schatz des liturgischen Chor- und Gemeindegesangs,* 3 vols., 1865–72.

24Winterfeld, Carl von. *Der evangelische Kirchengesang,* 3 vols., 1843–47.

25Friedrich Lochner (1822–1902), who at this time was pastor in Springfield, Ill., was sent to America in 1845 and became an important shaper of the liturgical life of the Missouri Synod. His writings include the *Passions- und Osterbuch, Liturgische Formulare,* and *Der Hauptgottesdienst der Ev. Luth. Kirche.*

26Walther, while serving Concordia Seminary in St. Louis at this time, also continued to supervise the four Saxon congregations in St. Louis, one of which was Holy Cross, the congregation at which Hoelter was serving.

27Conspicuously absent from this listing is the name of Karl Brauer, professor of music at the teacher-training school at Addison, Ill. Brauer had been listed as cooperating in the production of this *Choralbuch (Der Lutheraner,* XLI (Oct. 1, 1885), 151). Two years after the publication of Hoelter's *Choralbuch"* (1886), Concordia Publishing House published Karl Brauer's *Mehrstimmiges Choralbuch* (1888).

15

Mehrstimmiges Choralbuch[1]

Zu dem Kirchengesangbuch für Evangelisch-
Lutherische Gemeinden Ungeänderter
Augsburgischer Confession

Herausgegeben von Karl Brauer.[2] St. Louis, Mo.;
Concordia Publishing House, 1888.

Chorale Book in Several Voices

For the Church Hymnbook for Evangelical Lutheran
Congregations of the Unaltered Augsburg Confession

Edited by Karl Brauer. St. Louis, Mo.; Concordia Publishing
House, 1888.

Preface

By means of the second edition of the *Kern des deutschen
Kirchengesangs* of Dr. Fr. Layriz[3] one congregation after another
soon learned to sing the hymns according to the tunes that it
contained. These were pleasing because of their original, lively,
swinging rhythms and their melodies with their characteristic
settings. The longer these tunes were used, the more firmly they
became the heritage of the congregations of our synod.
Unfortunately, this edition soon went out of print and became
difficult to purchase. A third edition which appeared in 1854
frequently changed the earlier melodies and rhythms. But if
congregational singing is to become and remain firm and secure,
it is necessary to retain the initially established tune. It was

regrettable that there was now no collection of tunes in the form already familiar to the congregations. Therefore an abridgment of the second edition of the *Kern* of Layriz was welcomed with joy.[4] However, it had the shortcoming of including only a limited selection of tunes. Many a hymn in our hymnbook could be taught only according to a melody that was less suited to the meaning of the hymn than another tune which had already been in use in the Lutheran Church for a long time. The number of such tunes is not small. Besides, there are among them also tunes that are worthy to be learned where they are as yet unknown and preserved for our descendants.

For the promotion of congregational singing also among our descendants, it is necessary for the future pastors, cantors, and organists to adopt the hymn tunes, especially in our circles, in the form in which they have come into use through the years. To that end it is necessary to put into the hands of those who are preparing themselves for such service the most complete collection possible which they can afterwards use in the service of the congregations.

To produce a collection that corresponds to the present needs, the *Choralbuch* presented here complies with the desire and request of the directors of Concordia Publishing House and of the right honorable general president, H. C. Schwan.[5]

This book contains the 194 tunes referred to in our church hymnbook.[6] Only a few of those named in the hymnbook had to be omitted because in most cases they differed from those given here only in the title.

The second edition of the *Kern* of Layriz was used as the preferred source. Where this was inadequate, the following works were used:

Dr. Fr. Layriz, *Kern*, 3rd edition

Dr. Schöberlein, *Schatz des liturgischen Chor und Gemeindegesangs*

C. Winterfeld, *Der evangelische Kirchengesang. Nuünberg-isches Gesangbuch*, 1690

Hommel, *Liturgie*[7]

Dr. J. G. Herzog, *Choralbuch*, 1886

Works of J. Seb. Bach were also used.

When the typesetter had already gone ahead with a considerable portion of the work, two more valuable works came to my aid:

1. Hans Leo Hassler, *Psalmen und Geistliche Lieder*, 1608

2. Dr. Otto Kade, *Vierstimmiges Choralbuch*, 1886

Deviations in harmony from those in Layriz are based on settings from the 16th and 17th centuries.

An appendix begins with No. 195. It contains for the most part the tunes still missing for the "Hausgesangbüchlein" (*Gebetsschatz*). In addition, some tunes which already appear in the main section are included but are differently harmonized in the appendix. Furthermore, there are some melodies different from those in the main section but belonging to the same hymns. Finally, I thought I needed to include certain tunes although they cannot be numbered among the true church tunes. Among these are Nos. 228[9] and 239.[10] The first one already found acceptance in the "*Sing und Betbüchlein*" through the influence of the now sainted C. F. W. Walther. The latter is given a place here because (alas!) it has already replaced Luther's tune in many localities.

The fermata sign should not be regarded as such, but should rather serve only the express purpose of locating the verse lines more easily.

The hymns are arranged alphabetically. Those out of order are so placed by the typesetter to avoid awkward page turning.

For the glory of God alone and for the service of the kingdom of Christ!

Karl Brauer Addison, Illinois
the end of August, 1888

Notes

[1]This collection contained 194 settings plus 50 additional settings in an appendix. Later printings in 1897, 1900, 1903. and 1906 helped make its use widespread throughout The Lutheran Church—Missouri Synod.

A review of the *Choralbuch* in *Der Lutheraner*, XLIV (Oct. 9, 1888), 168, signed "A.G." gives the following reasons for the appearance of a new *Choralbuch* only two years after the publicaton by the same publisher of the *Choralbuch* edited by H. F. Hoelter: the new book contained fewer hymns and was therefore lower priced; in addition it had the advantages of a horizontal format rather than a vertical one, and it included hymns texts along with the music. A lengthy review in the *Ev.-Luth. Schulblatt*, XXIII (1888), 180–82, signed "K." [very likely D. A. W. Krauss, director of the Teachers' Seminary at Addison, Ill., where Brauer was professor of music] encourages its introduction into every church of the synod.

[2]Karl Brauer was born January 10, 1831, at Lissberg, Hessen. A graduate

of the Friedberg Teachers Seminary, he emigrated to America in 1850 and taught at the following elementary schools of The Lutheran Church—Missouri Synod: St. Johns, Philadelphia, Pa. (1850–54); Trinity, St. Louis, Mo. (1854–55); Zion, Cleveland, Ohio (1855–65); Baltimore, Md. (1865–66). From 1866–97 he was professor of music at the Addison Teachers Seminary. He retired to North Tonawanda, N.Y., where he died on May 12, 1907. He was the first prominent music instructor in the Missouri Synod. His writings include many articles on music, organs, and organ playing which appeared in the *Ev.-Luth. Schulblatt*, XLII (May 1907), 129. For a picture and address at his 25th anniversary, see Ibid., XXVII (January 1892), 1–13. Brauer's involvement and relationship to the publication two years earlier of Hoelter's *Choralbuch* is not clear. See footnote 27 of the Preface to the 1886 volume.

3Friedrich Layriz, *Kern des deutschen Kirchengesangs*. 4 vols. (Nördlingen: C. H. Beck'sche Buchhandlung, 1844-55.)

4This was the *Evangelisch-Lutherisches Choralbuch für Kirche und Haus* published 1863 in St. Louis, Mo., by Mr. L. Volkening, a private publisher. It contained 162 settings.

5Heinrich Christian Schwan (1819–1905) was born at Horneburg, Hanover. After his ordination in 1843, he took charge of a mission in Brazil. In 1850 he came to the United States and was installed as pastor in Black Jack, Mo. In 1851 he was called to Zion Church, Cleveland, Ohio, where he served until 1899. (It was at this church that Karl Brauer served as teacher from 1855–65.) From 1878 to 1899 Schwan served as president of the Missouri Synod.

6*Kirchengesangbuch für Evangelisch-Lutherische Gemeinden ungeänderter Augsburgischer Confession* (New York: Gedruckt für die Herausgeber bei H. Ludwig. Im Verlag der deutschen evang. luth. Gemeinde u. A. C. in St. Louis, Mo., 1847).

7Hommel, Friedrich, *Liturgie für Lutherischen Gemeindegottes- dienst*, 1851. A German (1813–92) who, through his acquaintance with Wilhelm Loehe, V. Tucher, and Fr. Layriz, came to know and appreciate the Lutheran music of the 16th and 17th centuries. His *Liturgie* was one of the texts used by Loehe in training his "Sendlinge" or missioners from Neuendettelsau to America in the mid-1800s.

8*Evangelisch-Lutherischer Gebetsschatz .... Nebst einem Hausgesang- büchlein*. St. Louis: Concordia Publishing House. Of the 45 hymns contained in the Appendix to Brauer's *Choralbuch*, 31 supply missing tunes for the "Hausgesangbuechlein."

9"Mein lieber Gott, ich bitte dich."

10"Wir glauben all an einen Gott." This tune which first appeared in a Ms. Choralbuch of Johann Gottlieb Wagner (1742), Langenoels, Schlesien, is found in countless chorale books throughout the 1800s. It is still found in *The Lutheran Hymnal* (No. 251, First Tune).

16

Church Book

The General Council, formed in 1867 as a result of dissension within the General Synod, was one result of the rising tide of confessionalism in American Lutheranism in the later 1800s. It published two hymnals, an English Church Book *(1868) and a German* Kirchenbuch *(1877). The* Church Book *was generally considered the best English Lutheran hymnbook that Lutherans in America had yet produced. The* Church Book with Music *(1872) was edited by Harriet Reynolds Krauth, daughter of Charles Porterfield Krauth, one of the leading theologians of the confessional revival.*

Church Book

For the Use of Evangelical Lutheran Congregations. By authority of the General Council of the Evangelical Lutheran Church in America

With Music,[1] Arranged for the use of Congregations by Harriet Reynolds Krauth.[2] Published with the Recommendation of the General Council. Philadelphia: Lutheran Book Store, 1872

Preface

In laying the Church Book with Music before the public, the Editor wishes to say something of the general plan and purpose of the work, and also to speak more particularly of certain points in it.

This book has grown out of a manuscript compilation, originally intended for one of our Mission Churches in Philadelphia, and to some extent used in it. The strictly congregational character of the first manuscript has been retained, in the belief that congregational singing, led by a choir or precentor, is the best mode for public worship, and most in keeping with the Service of our Church.

The Chants used in

The Liturgy

have been carefully selected from the best compilations. To these has been added music adapted from various sources, generally English or German, to suit the Kyries and Versicles. For many of these adaptions the Editor is responsible. For others, thanks are due to friends whose names are given with the music. Throughout this portion of the work, the music has been selected with regard to the unity of the Service, as well as to the varied requirements of the Church-Year. By a system of reference from each part of the Service to that which follows immediately, the abrupt changes which often mar liturgical worship are avoided, and a musical arrangement is secured, adapted in all its parts to the Seasons of the Church-Year.

In pointing the words for chanting, comparison has been made in every instance with the best English usage so far as the variations in the Psalter permitted, and this usage has been seldom departed from, except where the length of the Psalm or the structure of the Chant required a special treatment.

In adapting music to the

Translations from the German,

the Editor has endeavored to give to each of them its proper melody. The exceptions, real or apparent, to this rule are:

1st. When words have been written to a tune previously composed, which retains as its name the opening line of the hymn to which it was first set.

2d. When in translating or selecting a hymn, it has been so altered that the original metre is lost.

3d. When the proper tune was quite unsuited to the English ear, and could readily be replaced by a smoother melody.

4th. German usage could be determined.

Now that these melodies, so intimately associated with the life and history of our Church, are being eagerly sought out and adapted to the needs of other Protestant Churches, it is specially fitting that English Lutherans should, wherever possible, use Lutheran tunes in their proper form, lest by our wilful negligence this rich heritage should pass irrecoverably into the hands of strangers.

The harmonies of these tunes have been compared when possible with those given by Layriz, many of them being taken from the "Kern des Deutchen Kirchengesangs," Dr. Fr. Layriz, 1854. Others come from the "Chorale Book for England," edited by William Sterndale Bennett and Otto Goldschmidt, London, 1865.

The numerous English adaptations of Chorales have also furnished material for this portion of the book. When the change of melody has been very slight, it had been restored, and the harmony credited to the English composer. When the alteration has been more extensive, the tune is given with the English name, and in most cases the original Chorale indicated.

In a very few instances the Editor has slightly altered a tune rather than omit it entirely, as in Hymn 41, where the last line is lengthened in the translation.

In crediting the Chorales to their composers, the works named above have been taken as authority, for this book makes no claim to antiquarian research, or to the use of original sources. The Editor hopes, however, that by careful comparison of the reliable compilations used, accuracy on this point has been attained.

The greater part of the remaining hymns are set to

English Hymn Tunes.

In the selection of these the works of the Rev. Thomas Helmore, the Rev. W. H. Havergal, Dr. E. G. Monk, Dr. H. J. Gauntlett, Jas. Turle, John Hullah, the Rev. J. B. Dykes. and others, have been used.

The "Church Psalter and Hymn Book," edited by the Rev. William Mercer, M. A., (Oxford edition, 1864,) has supplied much of the material used, and in its general arrangement and

typography, suggested the form in which this volume appears.
The Editor has endeavored to make the

Indexes

a valuable feature of the book. The Alphabetical Index to the Liturgy is specially designed to aid that large class of worshippers who desire to take part in the entire service, but whose acquaintance with the contents of the Church Book is limited. The convenience of turning without difficulty to any Collect or Introit, will be appreciated by the Pastors also.

In the Alphabetical Index of Tunes an effort has been made to give as fully as possible the authorship and date of tunes, with occasional mention of other interesting points. Did space permit, this portion of the work could be almost indefinitely enlarged, the German tunes especially, having in many cases a history made beautiful by the Christian experience in which they have borne a part. In this Index the term "proper tune" implies either that the tune or adaptation was made for the words, or that it has come to be invariably used with them.

Believing that the use of the German Chorales in English congregations will be greatly facilitated by a more convenient system of naming, and at the same time deprecating the usual mode of attaching unmeaning titles to melodies, many of which have been linked for centuries with certain words, the Editor has given a translated title to each of them, adding an Index of the English names to the Alphabetical Index of Tunes. For these English titles, Miss Winkworth's translations have been generally used, but in some cases a literal rendering has been necessarily adopted.

The Metrical Index shows at a glance the key, pitch, and general character of each tune. Its construction, suggested by Layriz, is perhaps the most simple that could be devised, being based first on the number of lines in a verse, then on the number of syllables in a line, thus avoiding the inconvenience of the more artificial division into Iambic, Trochaic, and other metres. The "highest note in melody" varies only from the third line in the treble staff to the fifth line, F# being the highest note occurring in any melody.

The Editor would gratefully acknowledge the courtesies received from personal friends and others in the preparation of the work. Constant encouragement, as well as important aid and advice, have been given by the Rev. Jos. A. Seiss, D.D[3].; and the Editor of this work, in common with all who have at heart the interests of our Church music, must feel grateful to him for the self-sacrificing labor which did much in preparing the way for a fuller liturgical service, and in teaching our people the advantage of a music-book in the hands of the congregation.

Permission was given by Messrs F. J. Huntingdon & Co., New York, to use copyright tunes from the "Book of Common Praise;" and to the Editor of that work, the Rev. Wm. Staunton, D. D., thanks are due for valuable suggestions, as well as for the courtesy that facilitated successful application to his publishers.

Mr. J. Remington Fairlamb, author of "New Songs unto the Lord," (Pond & Co., 1864–5,) and Jas. Pearce, Mus. Bac. Oxon,. Organist of St. Mark's Protestant Episcopal Church, Philadelphia, allowed the unfettered use of their published works. The tune to hymn 435 is printed from the Author's MS., and most of the harmonies credited to Mr. Pearce, as well as the second tune to Hymn 578, are here published for the first time.

Permission was received from Mr. Henry L. Mattes, Organist of St. John's Lutheran Church, Easton, Pa., to use the manuscript Service arranged by him. From manuscripts of Mr. J. Muhlhauser, the Kyries and Versicles credited to him, are taken. The Editor would make grateful mention of all these gentlemen, as well as of friends who have aided the work by the suggestion and loan of material, and in other ways.

Thanks are due to Mr. Fairlamb for corrections and revisions of harmony in the manuscript on which this work is based. Still more assistance of the same kind has been rendered by Mr. Pearce in preparing the manuscript for the press, every page of which has been revised by him.

September 21st, 1872

Ye that stand in the house of the Lord, in the courts of the house of our God, Praise the Lord; for the Lord is good; sing praises unto His Name, for it is pleasant.

Thy Name, O Lord, endureth for ever; and Thy memorial, O Lord, throughout all generations.

Practical Suggestions

The importance of frequent meeting for congregational singing, cannot be too strongly urged upon Pastors. An hour in each week, given to the study and practice of church music, will soon enable any Congregation to join devoutly and intelligently in every portion of the Service.

In the Liturgy, the figures of reference are so arranged that from each Opening Versicle (Morning Service) or Invitatory (Ev. Serv.) any one of the Hymns of Praise may be reached, without marked change of key.

The Gospel Versicles, being arranged according to their signatures, require no figures. To inexperienced organists it may be well to suggest that the character of the Psalm as well as its signature, should be considered in choosing the Versicle to follow.

As the figures of reference are intended for the use of the Congregation, it is hoped that the organist will ordinarily find it convenient to follow the course indicated by them.

Where the directions on a page are separated by double lines, all above the lines are Rubrics "by authority." Those below the lines refer to the music, or are drawn from the Rubrics of the Church Book.

Where a Rubric "by authority" requires some addition in connection with the music, or in consequence of the partial rearrangement of the Church Book, this is given in a foot-note, or enclosed in brackets.

In the unbarred melodies, the most important of which is the Alleluiatic Sequence, 19a, the accent of the words determines that of the music. Bars are here only used to show the ending of the lines, and double bars, of the verses, of each hymn. It is seldom desirable to pause much (sometimes not at all) at the end of each line, especially when the sense of the words (or the structure of the melody) connects it with the following line of the hymn or phrase of the music. The slur connects two or more notes when they are to be sung to one syllable. Notes of the same value tied thus, should be sung in equal and measured time, and the half notes should bear the same relation to the whole notes as in other music.

Good taste, and a keen sense both of the poetic and musical

accent, will in general leave little doubt on the mind of the musician, as to what is the best reading of each particular melody; while the rate of progress will be dictated by its style and structure, the Season of the Church Year, the sentiment of the verse and the capabilities of the singer or accompanist.*

*From the Preface to "Accompanying Harmonies to the Hymnal Noted." Rev. Thos. Helmore, London, 1862

The same rule in regard to the rate of speed, will apply to all melodies German as well as English; the notation of these, whether in half notes or quarter notes, being chosen in every case for typographical reasons only.

Congregations unaccustomed to chanting will find the following explanation useful.

Chants are of two kinds, single and double. A single Chant is composed of two parts, the first consisting of three bars, and the last of four, and is to be sung through once to every verse of the Psalm or Introit.

A double Chant is exactly equal to two single Chants, and must be sung through once to every two verses. Should the Psalm contain an odd number of verses, the last half of the Chant should be repeated for the final verse, in order that the Gloria Patri may begin with the first strain.

In many cases a better mode of preventing the break is this: the organ gives the first half of the Chant, and the congregation begins the first verse upon the second half of the Chant. (See Psalm III.) The second and third verses are then sung to the complete Chant, and thus to the end. In the Psalm after the Epistle (or first Lesson) the Hallelujah may be sung to the first half of the Chant.

Good chanting is simply good reading, only in a musical tone; the grouping of the words, emphasis, expression, etc., should be the same as in reading. The first thing in the study of a Chant, therefore, is to determine upon the most natural and emphatic expression of the words. The time of the first or reciting note is variable, and must depend upon the number of syllables to be sung to it; but though it may be held longer than a full bar if the number of words require it, yet, however few the words, it is never held less than a full bar. These words should not be unduly hurried, but recited at the pace in which they would commonly be read.

A slight pause may be made upon the last accented word before the bar, but only such a pause as the emphasis would require in ordinary reading.

The first bar marks the beginning of musical time, which continues to the double bar, after which the recitation is resumed.

A single word or syllable between two bars, is to be sung to all the notes between the corresponding bars in the music.

Where more than two syllables occur in one bar, the accent of the words and music must coincide.

As a rule, the words "of the" "to the" and similar phrases, before or after an accented word in the same bar, are to be sung to one note.

A dot following a bar shows that the preceding syllable is still held. So two dots indicate that the notes of the whole bar are to be sung to the preceding syllable

Notes

[1]The 1872 *Church Book. . . with Music* contains 588 hymns with four-part harmonizations. All stanzas are grouped together below the musical staff. A metrical index of tunes lists the name of the tune, hymn numbers, the keys of the hymns, the highest note in the melody, and the character of the hymn (festive, solemn, general). The musical settings of the liturgy are set to Anglican chant. The melodies of the hymns are generally isorhythmic. The *Church Book*—without music—first appeared in 1868.

[2]Harriet Reynolds Krauth (1845–1925), the daughter of Rev. C. Porterfield Krauth and granddaughter of Rev. C. Philip Krauth, was married in 1879 to Rev. Adolph Spaeth (later president of the General Council) and was editor of the *Church Book with Music*. Her son, Sigmund Spaech, was a well-known writer on music. She spent many years translating German and Scandinavian texts into English, a number of which appeared in the *Church Book*.

[3]Joseph Augustus Seiss (1823–1904) was a Lutheran pastor who served in Baltimore and Philadelphia, a founder and later president of the General Council, editor of *The Lutheran* (1869–79), and a prolific author. He was particularly influential in helping to shape the liturgy of the *Church Book*.

17

Choral-Bog

The matter of the rhythmic chorale was an issue in the Norwegian church in the 19th century, both in Norway and in America. The three Forewords given here reflect aspects of that debate. Knud Henderson's Choralbog *(1866)—the first Norwegian music book published in America—was the first to champion the rhythmic form of the chorale in America. Erik Jensen's* Koralbog *(1879)—which followed the approach of Ludvig Lindeman in the treatment of the chorale as opposed to those advocating a return to the original rhythmic form—although a purely private venture, became the dominant book among Norwegians in America, at least until the turn of the century. The* Rhytmisk Koralbog *(1904), strongly influenced by Ulrik V. Koren, president of the Norwegian Synod (1894-1910), advocated the use of the original rhythmic form.*

Choral-Bog

Choral-Bog, indeholdene Melodier for de Norske og Svenske Psalmebøger, tilligemed en Musik Skole, 1866[1]

Chorale Book, containing melodies for the Norwegian and Swedish Hymnals, together with a Music School, 1866

Foreword

Norwegians in America have for a long time lacked a Norwegian chorale book, and this book is an attempt to fill that need.[2] There is hardly any national group in America among whom singing, both in church and at home, is at such a low ebb as it is generally among the Norwegians.[3] It would seem, therefore, that it is high time to try to restore to the old chorale melodies, in their splendid simplicity, the life which indifferent times have taken from them, especially since more frequent use of these melodies in church and home is surely the most effective means to awaken interest in our lethargic church music and lift it out of the doldrums in which it has been in the last years.[4] But in order to reintroduce the melodies in their original form one must first and foremost try to gain the understanding of the pastors, organists, precentors and school teachers in the hope that they will lend informed help. At the same time the chorale book should be used in schools and singing societies, where interest is most quickly aroused.[5] If one will pursue these courses diligently the effort to replace our sluggish, dull singing with fresh, expressive singing will soon begin to bear fruit.

This present edition includes a Method of Singing adequate to teach one to sing from notes. It includes also a sufficient number of melodies which are currently being used for our hymns. Among these melodies are major and minor melodies in the same meter. The small numbers immediately above the melodies refer to the number of syllables in each verse, and from them one can find different melodies usable with the same meter.

Most of the melodies are in the rhythm which they possessed originally, e.g. Nos. 26, 27, 28, 56, 57, etc. But other melodies, such as 20, 24, and 35, together with some others which are so well known in their iso-rhythmic form, I have not attempted to arrange in their original form, but have left them in the meter in which they are presently used.

I am not seeking, therefore, to introduce any new time or meter, but some of the old rhythms.

If one learns well to know the original melodies he will soon perceive that they have power to arouse the mind and express the heart's innermost and deepest feelings—something which our church music in late years has not been able to do. In many-voiced rhythmic singing there is life, power and warmth which will awaken in the young a renewed interest in attending church and singing schools, and which will be to the general edification of all.

A supplement will be forthcoming.[6]

K[nud]. H[enderson].

Notes

[1]This collection was the work of Knud Henderson (1835–1930), who was born in the Voss area of western Norway, emigrating with his family to America at the age of 14, settling on a farm just outside Cambridge, Wis. Two years later Knud left for Chicago, Ill., where he contracted for three years as an apprentice painter. A few years later he began studies in music in Chicago. Among his teachers were George F. Root for singing, for organ a representative of the Chant and Pincher Company of pipe organ builders, and for composition a Swede by the name of Edward Wimmerstedt, said to have been the earliest professional Swedish musician in Illinois (Ernst W. Olson, *The Swedish Church in Illinois*, Chicago, 1917, pp. 158–59). Root, in particular was a prominent 19th-century composer of such popular Civil War songs as "Just before the Battle, Mother" and "Tramp, Tramp, Tramp, the Boys are Marching."

Among his other music activities—in addition to his *Choral-Bog*—was the publication of a collection of secular songs, *National og Selskabs Sange* (Chicago, 1876). He also devised a method of playing the *salmodikon* by notes instead of numbers, and claimed to have built over 300 such instruments. He eventually moved back to the family home in Cambridge, Wis., where he died at the age of 95. For much of the information related to the Norwegian chorale books I am indebted to Gerhard Cartford, *Music in the Norwegian Lutheran Church: A Study of Its Development in Norway and Its Transfer to America, 1825–1917*. Thesis, University of Minnesota, 1961.

[2]This is the first Norwegian music book edited in America. Cartford points out, "When O. M. Norlie says on p. 54 of *Prominent Personalities* (Northfield, Minn., Mimeographed, 1942) that Ole Andrewson was the first to issue a music book among the Norwegian-Americans, he is referring to Guldberg's which Andrewson published in 1854." Andrewson's book, however, contained no music, only words.

[3]Each immigrant group could probably make a similar statement since the general state of congregational singing was, by the middle of the 19th century, at low ebb everywhere.

[4]Henderson was "the first to champion the rhythmic chorale among Norwegians in America." Exactly how and where he developed this interest is difficult to say. However, the very first chorale in this collection may give a hint: It is taken from Friedrich Layriz' *Kern des deutschen Kirchengesangs* (1844–55). Layriz had followers among the German Lutherans in St. Louis who also championed Layriz' collections and his cause.

Cartford notes: "The bulk of the first edition is made up of historic chorales of the Lutheran Church. But there are gaps where key segments of the literature are absent, e.g., the Kyrie hymn the creedal hymn (subsequently added); the Litany (subsequently added); the great Easter hymn, *Den Herre Krist i aødsens band* (Christ lag in Todesbanden); Luther's hymn on the Word of God, *Behold os Herre* (Erhalt uns Herr)—the text of which is here set to *Jesu dulcis memoria*." The collection was, nevertheless, a beginning at a return to the historic chorales among the Norwegians. By the 1873 edition, Henderson mentions "two editions having been sold out since 1866"—some 2,000 copies in all.

[5]The specific origin of this collection is of particular interest. Henderson conducted Norwegian "singing schools" in Chicago—one in a Hauge synod church, one in Pastor C. J. P. Pederson's church, and one in Pastor Jens I. Krohn's church. In the early 1860s Henderson was asked by some members of his choir to rearrange the settings they were using from O. A. Lindeman's chorale book which they felt were too difficult to sing. In complying with this request he began the efforts which resulted in his 1866 collection.

[6]Various supplemental additions were made in succeeding editions. Cartford notes that the organization of the first edition—a core of Lutheran chorales arranged alphabetically—breaks down as each succeeding edition adds supplements. The hymns added in later editions are a mixture of tunes from Lindeman's and Hoff's books, from the songs of Oscar Ahnfelt, a popular Swedish composer, together with compositions of his own and others. By 1873 Henderson had changed the title of his collection to *Koral-Bog, indeholdene Melodier for Salmer og sandelige Sange* (Chorale Book, containing Melodies for Hymns and Spiritual Songs), reflecting the changing nature of the contents.

18

Koralbog

Koralbog, indeholdene Melodier til Synodens, Landstads, Guldbergs o. fl. Salmebøger, samt til Salmer i det Engelske, for Orgel, blandet Kor eller Piano. Chicago, 1879.[1]

Chorale Book containing Melodies for the Synod, Landstad, Guldberg and other Hymnals, together with Hymns in English, for Organ, Mixed Choir or Piano. Chicago, 1879

Foreword

The present chorale book contains melodies for all the hymns in the Synod, Landstad and Guldberg hymnals, and also for those in the Hauge hymnal with the exception of about 20 hymns that will seldom, if ever, be used anyway. The book contains over 190 melodies, including a few English ones. A specific index also lists a number of our Lutheran melodies which are usable for the English hymns. Specifically, one can find tunes for 127 of the hymns in the *Hymn Book*[2] issued by The Lutheran Publishing House, Decorah, Iowa, in other words, the whole book except for hymns 80, 92, and 101. With the help of the metrical index one can easily find new melodies for hymns not listed in the alphabetical index. Likewise, one can substitute a melody for the one listed provided that the meter is identical. One should, however, take care that the melody fits the character of the hymn; for example, it would not do to sing Idag er Naadens Tid [This is the day of grace] to the melody *Nu takker alle Gud* [Now thank we all our God], or *O Ansigt høit forhaanet* [O sacred head now wounded] to the melody *Jeg vil mig Herren love* [I will praise the Lord], etc. If congregations and choirs do not know the melodies which best suit the hymns they should learn them, and in general strive to recapture the use of our Lutheran hymn tunes.

With regard to the choice of melodies, I have taken 147 in all from Lindeman's authorized book of melodies[3] to Landstad's hymnal, 27 from Hoff,[4] and 18 from other sources (see List of Sources, p. 151 ff.). Most of the melodies from Hoff and other books are melodies for hymns in the Synoden and Hauge hymnals which are not found in Lindeman. In general I have tried to use the best of our Lutheran church music insofar as it lends itself to use with the hymnals we have here. For this reason I have used Lindeman as a primary source, since I have not found another chorale book as satisfying as his.[5] This has also made possible a close tie with the music of the mother church. In many instances, as did Lindeman and Hoff, I have set 2 alternative melodies under one number, especially where too many hymns, or hymns of different character, have been sung to one melody. On the other hand, I have excluded some melodies, especially those old ones which are seldom used and which could be used only with difficulty alongside the better tunes which have been set to the same hymns, since the inclusion of such tunes would have lengthened the book unnecessarily and made more difficult the choice of the better and more usable tune. In view of the musical shortcomings of our present situation it seems unwise that a chorale book designed for congregational use should have too large a number of tunes. Furthermore, in future editions of this book there will be opportunity to make appropriate changes or additions suggested by usage.

It will be seen that almost without exception, I have used the harmony given with a melody, especially in the case of Lindeman. Since a melody can be harmonized in many different ways, if one follows the right rules, it follows that an organist, possessed of the necessary musical knowledge and skill, may, depending upon circumstances, change harmonies within a hymn—even on each stanza—for the sake of variety. However, if the organist is not skilled, or if a choir is singing the hymn in parts, the harmony must be played as written.

It should be understood, but perhaps needs emphasis, that no one in the congregation may sing parts different from those rendered by the organ or choir.

In only a few instances have I ventured further than

Lindeman in adopting the old rhythmic form of the chorale. A congregation is, and always will be, unmusical on the whole. For this reason it would have difficulty singing the syncopations and alternating duple and triple rhythms found in so many of our old church hymns. These rhythmically alternating hymns, so highly praised by some, were probably not originally as full of life and beauty as some people maintain. The original rhythmic forms should be used for a congregation only when the rhythm is even and in general natural and easy for the congregation to learn. Otherwise, the chorales in their original rhythm should be regarded as art music.[6]

I have not been able to accept the idea that we should adopt the original form of the chorale, set out by Layriz,[7] in order to work together with our German brothers-in-the-faith against the day that we forsake our mother tongue and unite as an English-speaking church. In the first place, the majority of the German Lutherans in this country probably do not use Layriz, or, for that matter, the original form at all, and of those who do use it there are surely very few congregations (in any case, only larger city congregations and those places where there are schools) where the rhythmic versions are sung reasonably correctly. In most instances, one will be forced after a while to give up the exact original rhythmic form as unnatural and impractical and adopt a more natural form. However, the form which the melodies have taken in the Norwegian church, with regard to both meter and melody, are without doubt preferable to the original and, consequently, ought not to be given up. Finally, in order not to run our own church music here completely into the ground, we must, in view of the shortcomings of our schools, preserve the customary form insofar as possible.

I did not think it expedient to give both forms of the chorale, i.e. the rhythmic and isorhythmic [*koral-form*], and thus leave the choice open. Most people are not equipped to choose the best, and in any case this would only cause regrettable confusion in our music since some would choose the first form and others the second. Therefore, I have given only one form, but tried to choose the more appropriate.

It is unfortunately true that our church music in general is far from what it ought to be. Everything possible ought to be done so our singing can be more vital and better serve its purpose. We ought to sing in faster tempo and with more life that we usually do (of which more later). And the melodies which cannot be easily sung by the congregation in their original form should where possible be edited to give them more life. In the final analysis, there probably is no more effective means to achieve this than the dotted notes which Lindeman used, which was to some extent used by older church musicians, and which preserves the customary melodic form and leaves the meter unchanged and simple. This dotted rhythm, which Lindeman has used for a long time and which in his authorized chorale book is recommended for use all over Norway, consists in lengthening a note by means of a dot "in order to enliven the melody and clarify sentence and period structure." This form I have adopted in detail from Lindeman. It would be well if the schools and singing societies would practice these dotted rhythms; then it might be possible after a time to use them also in church where they could become familiar to the congregations. But the organist and the singing teacher must take care to see that these notes are performed exactly as written, metrically, at the same time as they are given the proper dignity and calm delivery necessary to religious music. Thus ♩ ♪ taken together, equal 4 eighth notes, i.e. 3 on the first note. Those who cannot render a dotted note with the necessary exactness and ease, or who prefer the usual method of playing, or who perhaps consider as unchurchly the more animated figures of music, may ignore the dotted values and play the notes in the customary way with equal length notes.

The melodies should be performed in strict time and not slower than will clearly differentiate the heavy from the light beats. Downbeat and upbeat (thesis and arsis) should have the proper stress—faster in the melodies with frequent long notes that have the alla breve signature, ¢, than in the rest with the usual C, or 4/4, signature. Melodies in triple meter are usually livelier and ought to be performed faster than those in duple meter. According to Lindeman's suggestion and practice, which ought to be followed, a quarter note should receive from 1-1 1/2 seconds, or thereabouts, faster or slower depending on the nature of the hymn, the music or the meter. To get a feeling for the tempo one can hang 2 strings from the ceiling, each with a weight at the lower end, one 40 and one 90 American inches long from ceiling to end of weight. Then, while you sing, set the weight to swinging and sing a quarter note for each swing. The 40 inch string will swing once a second, the 90 inch string once each second and a half. These should generally be the outer limits of the speed. One should never go slower than the slowest speed indicated above but rather aim for the faster limit, occasionally in 3/4 meter going a bit faster than that.*

*It would be desirable for both choir directors and precentors to study singing. I take the liberty of directing attention to my singing method in *Sangbog for Børn og Ungdom* (Songbook for Children and Youth), especially par. 2, 3, 5, 6, and 7. [Published in Chicago, 1878].

A rest is introduced at the end of a sentence for the purpose of drawing breath. This takes the place of the fermata formerly used in the old chorales (and much abused, especially in dragging out the final cadence). However, it is not necessary to break in all 4 voices. The top voice may be held for the full quarter note value, especially with full organ, while the lower voices drop out and observe the rest.

The chorales should be played in the strictest legato, including the notes connected without breaks. The bass line, however, is an exception to this rule. When clarity demands that the downbeat or accent (thesis) should be marked, the preceding note in the bass should be shortened, thus ♪ ⁊ | ♩ instead of ♩|♩.

Another exception occurs in dotted notes when the melody will not be clearly heard entering on the eighth note if the bass has the same note. In this case the bass line should read thus: ♩ ⁊ ♪ rather than ♩.♪ .

Since the chorales are written for four voices: discant [or soprano], alto, tenor and bass, the distribution of the four parts between the two hands on the piano or organ must be suited to the player. Thus, since the tenor voice is highest on the bass staff, he will occasionally have to play it with his right hand rather than his left. Likewise, in order to play more easily, he may occasionally play the bass notes an octave higher.

The whole congregation should take part in the liturgical responses found at number 171.

A good four-voiced choir to lead congregational singing is a beautiful and priceless thing. But it should always be borne in mind that the purpose of a church choir is to contribute to the general edification of the congregation and more particularly to aid congregational singing. This purpose should determine the nature of its music and its manner of performance. In a church choir the melody should be sung so prominently—especially when the organ is also playing—that the congregation can clearly hear it and follow along. It must never be forgotten that the singing of the congregation is of primary importance here. The choir's function is merely to serve this end.

Would that this book might serve to teach the congregation rightly to value and use our wonderful Lutheran church melodies and hymns, and that our young people and our descendants in this land would accept with love this heritage of costly jewels. Eph. 5:19; Col. 3:16. The blessing of God be shed upon this book, for Jesus' sake.

Jefferson Prairie parsonage
(Clinton P. O., Rock County, Wis.)
in October 1879

E[rik]. Jensen[8]

Notes

[1] This collection includes a detailed and informative foreword, carefully edited settings of 192 melodies, together with metrical and alphabetical indexes, an index of tunes for the English hymns in the 1879 hymnal, and a list of the sources of the melodies. Of the 192 melodies, 147 are taken from Lindeman, 27 from Hoff, and 18 from other sources—ten of these from the *Church Book with Music* (Philadelphia, 1872) edited by Harriet Reynolds Krauth.

A supplement of 16 melodies was added in 1882, and a second, and more important one, in 1895 containing 31 tunes—first published separately and then later bound into the book—was entitled *Tillaeg til Lindemans Koralbog, indeholdene Melodier til ny optagne Salmer og Sange i Salmebog for lutherske Kristne i America, eller Landstads Salmebog med Tillaeg* (Minneapolis, 1895) [Supplement to Lindeman's Chorale Book, containing Melodies for the recently added Hymns in Hymnal for Lutheran Christians in America, or, Landstad's Hymnal with Supplement].

Jensen's *Koralbog* was a purely private venture, never receiving official endorsement by any synod. Yet it was widely used and became the dominant book among Norwegians for the next twenty years. Although it was an advocate of Ludwig Lindeman's approach to the problem of the rhythmic chorale as opposed to those advocating a return to the original rhythmic forms, it was even used—together with other books—in the Washington Prairie Church in Iowa, the home congregation of Ulrik Koren, President of the Synod (1894-1910) and one of the most persistent and vocal champions of the rhythmic chorale, the congregation where his daughter Marie was organist for some 52 years.

[2] *Hymn Book for the use of Evangelical Lutheran Schools and Congregations* (Decorah, Iowa, 1879). This collection contained only texts.

[3] L. M. Lindeman, *Koralbog, indeholdene de i Landstads Salmebog forekommende Melodier* (Christiana, 1877).

[4] Erik Hoff, *Melodibog til samtlige authoriserede Salmebøger—Hauges, Landstads, evangelisk-kristelige, Guldbergs og Kingos, samt til "Salmebog for*

den norsk-evangelisk-lutherske Kirche i Amerika" (Kristiana, 1878).

5 It is clear from the contents of this collection as well as from statements such as this that Jensen cast his lot with Lindeman in matters regarding the rhythmic chorale.

6 Jensen's argument that the chorale in its original form is really art music and had best be left to the choir rather than the congregation was also Lindeman's argument expressed in his *Martin Luthers aandelige Sange* (Christiana, 1859). Only two years earlier, in the foreword to his *Sangbog for Børn og Ungdom* (1878), Jensen expressed the opposite view, although he gives no reasons for his apparent change of heart.

7 Friedrich Layriz, *Kern des deutschen Kirchengesangs zum Gebrauch evangelisch-lutherischer Gemeinden und Familien* (Noerdlingen, 1844-55).

8 Erik Jensen (1841-1927) was born in Norway, studied at the teachers' seminary at Asker, and then taught for six years before emigrating to America. He studied at Concordia Seminary, St. Louis, Missouri, and was ordained in 1870, serving parishes in Wisconsin for 22 years. In 1893 he was ousted from his parish as a result of a congregational dispute. He took up the Anti-Missourian cause and fought a twenty-year battle with the United church, living to the age of eighty-six. In his later years he was able to live from the proceeds of his writing, lecturing, and music publications, among which are his *Sangbog for Børn og Ungdom* (Chicago, 1878), *Scandinavian Songs, Part I* (Decorah, 1886) [Part II never appeared], *Børneharpen* (1889-1894), *Sange til Børneharpen* (1890), *Religiøse Korsange for Mandsstemmer* (1894), *Klokketoner* (1896), and *De Unges Sangbog* (1899).

19

Rhytmisk Koralbog

Decorah, Iowa. Lutheran Publishing House, 1904[1]

Rhythmic Chorale Book. Decorah, Iowa. Lutheran Publishing House, 1904

Foreword

The strong desire to issue a chorale book in rhythmic form has been expressed from various quarters. Where this form has been tried hymn singing has shown vitality hitherto unknown, and those who have experienced this would not return to the old sluggish method of singing which came into the church with rationalism.

In the days when the Lutheran church received the name "the singing church," it was the rhythmic form of the chorales that was used, and it was the congregations that sang.

The church council, therefore, instructed the synod's president[2] to select a committee[3] to draft such a chorale book. Since there was no one among us, as far as we knew, who had the necessary musical and historical qualifications to work out a new, independent book,[4] it was decided, after consultation with other interested parties, to investigate as far as possible what had already been done by competent people in other Lutheran churches and to make the best possible choices from these books.[5] It was not our purpose to get something new but to use what had been given to the church by musically qualified authorities in different Lutheran countries.

The committee, therefore, investigated as diligently as they were able what was to be found in recognized German, Danish, Norwegian and American chorale books such as the German collections of J. Zahn and J. G. Herzog, the Danish of Thomas

Laub, the Norwegian of L. M. Lindeman and E. Hoff and the German-American of H. F. Hoelter and J. Endlich, besides different American chorale books. In addition were assembled a small number of English hymn tunes for use where needed.

It will perhaps be said in many places that the melodies in this form are unsingable because they are so difficult that the congregations cannot learn them.[6] But what has been done elsewhere, e. g., in Germany, Denmark, and America, can certainly be done also among us, provided one does not begin with a negative attitude and the preconceived idea that "it just won't work." We have experienced that when one has sung the melodies a few times in this form he will like them and will realize that he never before knew how much was contained in these old hymn tunes.

Most of the melodies are given in the form in which we know them, except for the rhythm. A couple, which could not be found in rhythmic form, have been given a rhythmic form by the committee. In a few places the text has had to be adjusted slightly. A few of the melodies have been set lower to make them easier to sing.

Some of the melodies have the so-called "alternating rhythms," and would not fit into the usual metrical divisions without having the melody overlap the bar line, thereby making the hymn harder to read. They have been set here in keeping with their own rhythm. In this way they should cause no difficulty. One simply gives each note its alloted value. With regard to the tempo of the hymns one must try to adjust it to the character of the contents of hymn and melody—not too slow, but then not too fast either; nor should one feel that because a melody has many half notes in it it should be sung like a funeral hymn.

Where the signature is ₵ the half note gets the value of a quarter note with a C signature.

The songs which are gathered in a supplement are for the most part hymns which have been set for four-voiced part singing. There are few things that a congregation gets more joy [hygge] out of than this; but it goes without saying that such songs must not take the place of congregational singing, and that they, therefore, are usable only for the choir.[7]

In the historical information about the melodies, taken from the best sources available, stress has been laid on showing, (1) when the melodies were written or taken into church use, and

(2) the source for the setting used in this chorale book. Where it was not possible to say definitely who wrote the melody, its date only has been entered, when it was known.

The committee acknowledges with thanks the willingness with which such an authority in hymnody as Thomas Laub in Copenhagen has allowed the use of his works [arrangements] and composed new melodies for this book. Likewise, thanks are due the Concordia Publishing House, St. Louis, The John Anderson Publishing Company and the Engberg-Holmberg Co., Chicago, The Century Company, New York, and the Oliver Ditson Co., Boston, all of whom have allowed use of chorales from their publications.

The committee hopes that they have not unwittingly encroached upon any rights. If this should have happened it is hoped that the committee will be informed so that the matter can be righted.

On behalf of the committee,
Marie Koren[8]
August 1903

Notes

[1] The collection is divided into three parts. The first contains the Sunday and ordination liturgy; the second, the chorale settings, of which there were 157 titles, a few having two settings; and third, 34 selections for choir, including several Bach chorales and a Palestrina motet.

[2] Ulrik Vilhelm Koren (1826-1910) became president of the Norwegian Synod in 1894, serving for sixteen years until his death. Koren was born in Bergen, Norway, was educated and later taught at a Latin School, Christiana, emigrated to the United States in 1853 when he was ordained and served as pastor in Little Iowa (later Washington Prairie) and adjoining congregations near Decorah, Iowa (1853-1910). He taught briefly at Luther College (1874-75) and served as President of the Synod for the Norwegian Evangelical Lutheran Church in America (1894-1910).

Koren was a strong advocate of the use of the rhythmic chorale for congregational singing, in part, no doubt, because of his great friendship and regard for Johan D. Behrens, one of the great Norwegian advocates for a return to the use of the rhythmic form of the chorale. This placed Koren at odds with Ludvig Lindeman, a fact reflected in Marie Koren's recollection that at Washington Prairie "We used the chorale books of Jensen and Laub and H. F. Hoelter . . . but never Lindeman." (See Cartford, p. 212.) Koren had also opposed the introduction of texts by Nicolai Grundtvig because of his suspect theology. Thus it was not until 1903 that Grundtvig's *Kirken den er at gammelt Hus*, probably his most famous hymn text, appeared in the Synod's revised hymnal together with Lindeman's melody which he had written for that text in 1840.

3 Koren assembled a committee consisting of himself, his daughter Marie Koren, Pastors J. W. Preus, M. Fr. Wiese, A. K. Sagen, and Rasmus Malmin. Preus, Wiese, and Sagen were all graduates of Concordia Seminary, St. Louis, Missouri, and were acquainted with the Missouri Synod where H. F. Hoelter and Karl Brauer, followers of Friedrich Layriz, were also advocating a return to the original rhythmic form of the chorale.

A quarter of a century earlier in 1870 the Norwegian Synod had published its new hymnal. Prominent members of the committee were Ulrik Koren and Nils Brandt. Soon after work began on a chorale book with the appointment in 1875 of Nils Brandt—an instructor in music at Luther College, Decorah, Iowa—as chairman of the Chorale Book Committee. Apparently Erik Jensen was also a member of this committee, whose work came to naught, most likely because of the "theological wars" of the time. In 1894 Koren became President of the Norwegian Synod. In 1903 a revision of the synod hymnal appeared. Koren was convinced it was time for a new chorale book for the revised hymnal, this time one that would return to the use of the rhythmic form of the chorale.

4 The one man who did indeed possess both the musical and historical qualifications was the Synod's leading musician, John Dahle. Koren, however, felt that Dahle would be unsympathetic to his and the committee's point of view and would create an imbalance on the committee that would jeopardize its work. Dahle, some years later, would write what amounted to a hymnal companion for *The Lutheran Hymnary* which appeared in 1913.

5 The main books consulted were those of Johannes Zahn, Thomas Laub, Ludvig M. Lindeman, Erik Hoff, H. F. Hoelter, and J. G. Herzog.

6 It is clear from the argument here that the introduction of the rhythmic form of the chorale was not without its opposition.

7 This is in line with the idea of the revival of the rhythmic form of the chorale that the congregation sang in unison and that part-singing was reserved for the choir.

8 While this Foreword is signed by Marie Koren it was more likely written by her father Ulrik. In a draft of the Foreword which Cartford found among the Koren papers in the archives of the Koren Library at Luther College, Decorah, Iowa, it is clear that the chief author is Ulrik V. Koren himself, the President of the Synod. In a conversation with Marie in 1961 Cartford recounts that Marie indicated that her name appears because her father had said someone's name should, "so they put mine down." She also indicated in conversation with Cartford that the committee met informally, usually in a home, and that she would play the tunes as they were discussed.

20

The Lutheran Hymnary[1]

The first Lutheran hymnal to appear in the 20th century as a result of the movement toward consolidation and consensus was The Lutheran Hymnary *(1913), the result of the cooperative work among the three major Norwegian churches: the United Norwegian Lutheran Church, the Norwegian Lutheran Church, and the Hauge Lutheran Synod. Four years later, in 1917—the 400th anniversary of the Reformation—the three cooperating churches merged to form The Norwegian Lutheran Church of America (later the Evangelical Lutheran Church). The hymnal committee was headed by John Dahle with F. Melius Christiansen serving as music editor.*

Minneapolis: Augsburg Publishing House, 1913

Preface

The compilation of "The Lutheran Hymnary" is the work of a Joint committee of 12 members,[2] four of whom were appointed by the United Norwegian Lutheran Church,[3] four by the Norwegian Lutheran Synod,[4] and four by the Hauge Lutheran Synod.[5] Few changes in the personnel of the committee have been made during the four years in which it has been at work on the hymnal.

The considerations that prompted the creation of the joint committee were, chiefly, the common need of an adequate and satisfactory English hymn book; the fact of a common faith and confession as well as a common inheritance of Lutheran hymnody; the probability of getting a better hymn book through united endeavor than by separate effort; and, finally, the desirability of a common hymnary, especially in the event of a union of the Church bodies concerned.[6]

Prior to the organization of the joint committee, the United Church had for some years, through a committee, been engaged in compiling a new English hymn book; the Norwegian Synod had been similarly engaged. Thus the joint committee, when it set out upon its work, had the result of the labors of these two individual committees to begin with. It also had, in "The Christian Hymns"[7] of the Norwegian Synod and "The Church and Sunday School Hymnal"[8] of the United Church, a nucleus for the proposed joint hymn book.

It has been the constant aim and effort of the committee to embody in "The Lutheran Hymnary" the best translations of German[9] and Norwegian Lutheran hymns. Seventy-two hymns from the Norwegian and Danish familiar to our Norwegian-Danish Church people, from Landstad's[10] and the Synod[11] hymn books, appear in this collection for the first time in English dress.

The Norwegian Lutheran Church of America has inherited a rich treasury of hymns and chorals from the Mother Church; and while the Norwegian-American Church would secure this treasure and transmit it to her children, it is also hoped that the hymns of Kingo,[12] Grundtvig,[13] Brorson,[14] Landstad, Brun[15] and others, rendered into English, may prove attractive to the English bodies of the Church of the Reformation, and eventually find a place in their hearts and hymnals.[16]

Another feature of the present collection is its large number of distinctively Lutheran chorals. The committee has, in general, observed the principle of retaining the tune with which the hymn is associated. When, however, it has been found that a tune is lacking in churchliness or appropriateness for congregational singing, the committee has given the hymn a standard Lutheran choral. These chorals have survived the test of time and have proven their vitality and intrinsic value by long and constant use in the homes and sanctuaries of the people of God.

Twenty German chorals are arranged in rhythmical meter; twenty have a melodic or contrapuntal setting. These special features the committee hopes will serve a purpose in discovering the wish of the Church regarding the rhythmical form and the melodic arrangement of Lutheran chorals.[17]

It is hoped that the arrangement of the hymns according to Sunday texts of the church year, a feature familiar from our

Norwegian hymn books, will prove a valuable aid in selecting appropriate hymns for the services, and, better than a mere topical index, serve to promote a general use of the hymns found in the hymnal.[18]

It is due to add that, thanks to the very extensive hymnological library and hymnological knowledge and patient research of Rev. Carl Doving, late of New York City, and for the last year a member of the committee, many excellent translations of well-known German Lutheran hymns, translations made mostly by prominent English hymnologists,[19] have been secured for "The Lutheran Hymnary;" these translations have not appeared in an English Lutheran hymn book before.

Grateful acknowledgment is made to the Concordia Publishing House of St. Louis, Mo., for permission to use the music of the second Morning and Evening Service.

Grateful acknowledgment is also due to the many who, either in an official capacity or personally, have rendered the committee valuable aid by suggestions, translations or criticisms. A true hymnal cannot be made to order; it is not an artificial production. It develops out of the consciousness of the Church itself. The committee has not felt that its duty was to make a new hymn book, but only to make out of the vast treasury of Lutheran hymnody such a collection of genuine Lutheran hymns and chorals as should satisfy Lutheran Church people.

Finally, it is the prayer of the committee, that "The Lutheran Hymnary" may prove no small factor in the efforts made to unify the various Norwegian Lutheran Church bodies of our land.[20]

THE COMMITTEE
September, 1912

Notes

[1]The hymnal contained 618 hymns and 14 doxologies. Also included were two Morning and two Evening services, some Litanies, the Introits and Collects for the Church Year, and selected Psalms.

2The Committee was headed by John Dahle with F. Melius Christiansen serving as music editor. John Dahle (b. 1853) attended several of the Norwegian Lutheran colleges and seminaries in Minnesota. In 1903 he organized the Choral Union of the Norwegian Synod. Besides his work on this hymnal, Dahle edited many choir books and wrote choir music.

F. Melius Christiansen (1871–1955) emigrated to the United States in 1888. He studied at Augsburg College, Northwestern Conservatory of Music in Minneapolis, and the Royal Conservatory of Music in Leipzig. He was head of the Music Department at St. Olaf College from 1903–1943. The famed St. Olaf Lutheran Choir was organized by Christiansen in 1912.

3The United Norwegian Lutheran Church was formed in 1890 as the result of a merger by the Norwegian Augustana Synod, the Norwegian Danish Conference, and the Anti-Missourians. This synod was considered to be theologically in the middle of the road between the other two synods working on this hymnal. It was the largest of the three synods as in 1898 it had 1,059 congregations with 123,000 communicant members.

4The Norwegian Lutheran Synod was formed in 1853. It was the bulwark of conservatism among Norwegian Lutherans in America. In 1898 there were 735 congregations and 66,000 communicants.

5The Hauge Lutheran Synod exemplified Lutheran Pietism and sprang from the teachings of layman Hans N. Hauge, (1771–1824). Low-church Haugean immigrants were led in America by layman Elling Eielsen (1804–83). The Hauge Lutheran Synod itself was formed in 1875–76. By 1898 there were 217 congregations with 17,483 communicant members.

6Since 1905 these three synods had been working together toward a possible merger.

7*Christian Hymns for Church, School, and Home.* Decorah Lutheran Publishing House, 1898. This hymnal contained 309 hymns as well as an Order of Morning Service, Evening Service, and Sunday School Service. In this English hymnal there were only nine hymns translated from Scandinavian sources.

8*The Church and Sunday School Hymnal,* also of 1898, contained 316 hymn texts with only two being translated from the Norwegian. Supposedly this was because of the lack of adequate translations.

9About one-third of the hymns are German in origin.

10Magnus B. Landstad (1802–80) was a Norwegian Lutheran pastor, hymnwriter, and compiler of hymnbooks. Landstad's *Psalmebog* of 1869 was brought to America by many immigrants. In 1893 the three synods mentioned above joined in the publication of Landstad's hymnal, adding 96 hymns to make a total of 730.

11In 1874 the Norwegian Lutheran Synod had published its own *Psalmebog* in Norwegian.

12Thomas Kingo (1634–1703) was an outstanding Danish Lutheran hymnwriter. He liberated Danish hymnody from German domination. Some of his hymns are "Print Thine Image Pure and Holy," "He that Believes and is Baptized," and "Praise to Thee and Adoration."

13Nikolai P. Grundtvig (1783–1872) was a Danish Lutheran hymn writer and church leader. At first he was a strong fighter for orthodox Lutheranism. Later he placed the Apostol's Creed above the Bible claiming it had been given to the church by Christ Himself. He wrote many hymns covering every phase of Christian life. They include "Built on the Rock the Church Doth Stand" and "God's Word is Our Great Heritage."

14Hans A. Brorson (1694–1764) was another outstanding Danish Lutheran hymn writer. A staunch adherent of Pietism, he thus incurred the hostility of many orthodox pastors. His hymns include "Behold a Host Arrayed in White".

15Johann N. Brun (1745–1816) was a Norwegian Lutheran bishop and poet. His hymns are considered unrivaled in Norwegian poetry. In a literary feud in 1785 over reform in the order of public worship, he emerged as a foe of the spirit of the Enlightenment and was for the rest of his life an eloquent advocate of Lutheran orthodoxy, in constant opposition to the current ideas of his age.

16To this end, 262 translations were here included from Danish-Norwegian sources.

17The committee also attempted to discover a preference by including seven German chorales in both the rhythmic and the iso-rhythmic settings. These seven are the following: *Allein Gott in der Hoeh, Es ist gewisslich, Freu dich sehr, Herzlich tut mich, O Welt, ich muss dich lassen, Kommt her zu mir,* and *Wer nur den lieben Gott.* Of the chorales included in this hymnal, most are found in the iso-rhythmic form.

18In this unusual feature the hymns for the church year are arranged not only by Season, but by the Sunday or Festival in the Season. Thus one or more hymns have been chosen for every Sunday in the church year and are so indicated at the top of each page.

19These hymnologists include Catherine Winkworth, Richard Massie, and John Wesley.

20This prayer was answered when in 1917 these three synods, after years of discussions, united to form the Norwegian Lutheran Church of America.

21

Common Service Book and Hymnal of the Lutheran Church

The Common Service Book and Hymnal *(1917), which appeared on the 400th anniversary of the Reformation, was the result of work on a new hymnal which followed the agreement on the Common Service in 1888. The participating groups were the General Council, the General Synod, and the United Synod of the South. In 1918, the year following the publication of the* Common Service Book and Hymnal, *these three groups merged to form the United Lutheran Church in America.*

Common Service Book and Hymnal of the Lutheran Church

Copyright, 1917, by The General Synod of the Evangelical Lutheran Church in the United States of America, The Trustees of the General Council of the Evangelical Lutheran Church in North America, The United Synod of the Evangelical Lutheran Church in the South

Preface to the Common Service Book, 1917

The *Common Service Book of the Lutheran Church* contains the standard revised text of *The Common Service* of 1888,[1] newly edited Orders for Occasional Services, and other matter of a liturgical nature. It has been prepared by authority of the

General Bodies that authorized *The Common Service*, and is accompanied by a Common Hymnal.[2]

The Committee was instructed to follow, as far as possible, the Rule under which the text of *The Common Service* was originally prepared.[3] It has endeavored to be faithful to the spirit of the Rule, but in the preparation of the Orders for Occasional Services, has been obliged to accept the responsibility that rests upon the Church of every time and place, of adapting all its regulations to the purpose of edification.

In the compilation of The Hymnal, the Committee has sought to include the largest possible number of the classical hymns of the Church of all lands and times, particularly those that were produced in the age and by the spirit of the Protestant Reformation.[4] It has applied the standards of literary merit and extent of usage to all hymns, but the final test has been that of agreement with the faith and spirit of the Lutheran Church.[5]

The Hymnal differs in its structure from preceding English Lutheran Hymnals in the fact that it has been prepared in complete harmony with the spirit of the Liturgy and with the evangelical principle of the Church Year. In this it returns, after more than a century, to the plan adopted by Henry Melchior Muhlenberg in the first American Lutheran Hymnal (1786).

At no time in the history of the Lutheran Church has a Liturgy and Hymnal been provided of such comprehensive character and for use over such a wide extent of territory. The favor which *The Common Service* has enjoyed, even outside the Bodies that authorized it, awakens the hope that *The Common Service Book* may sooner or later meet the needs of the entire Lutheran Church in America.

Thus this Book, put forth during the Quadricentennial Year of the Reformation, witnesses to the essential strength and spiritual oneness of the Lutheran Church in America, and is a fruit of the desire for closer approach to common standards in its devotional life and usages.

Whitsuntide, 1917

The Music of the Book

In the selection of The Music the principle of a consensus of historic usage has been steadily kept in view and every effort has been made to furnish a setting worthy of the text.

The first setting of the Services is largely based on melodies long associated with the English text of the Liturgy, but in many cases antedating the Reformation; and compiled and edited for this Book by the Reverend J. F. Ohl,[6] Mus. Doc. Modern Anglican chants and arrangements of recognized value are also included.

The second setting contains the historic Plain Song melodies, most of which have had unbroken usage in the Christian Church for a thousand years or more. These melodies are given in their original unbarred form, as found in Archer and Reed, *The Choral Service Book*, 1901.[7] They should be sung in unison and in a free rhythm determined by the flow and accent of the text.[8]

The music of the hymns has been chosen from a wide range of sources, from the ancient Plain Song, German and Scandinavian Chorale melodies, French, Swiss, Scotch and English Psalters, and from English and American composers of all periods. The effort has been made to select melodies that have borne the test of time and wide usage and which are best adapted to congregational use. For translations of hymns the melodies associated with the originals have been used whenever possible, the Chorale melodies in most instances in their rhythmic form.

Tunes which have been especially composed for this book are marked with a cross (+) and should not be reprinted without permission.

The hearty thanks of the Church are hereby extended to all who have written or translated hymns or composed tunes for this book. If any hymn or tune has been included for which proper credit is not given, it is with the regret of the Committee, as every effort has been made to communicate with living authors and composers whose hymns and tunes, already published elsewhere, have been included in the book, and to secure permission for their use.

Whitsuntide, 1917

Notes

[1]This volume included a reprint of the "Preface to the Common Service, 1888," which clearly reflected the bases for liturgical renewal current in American Lutheranism in the latter nineteenth century.

[2]The emergence and widespread acceptance of the *Common Service* (1888) provided the impetus for further joint work by the three church bodies that had worked toward its completion: the General Synod, the General Council, and the United Synod of the South. The hymns of the General Synod's *Book of Worship* (1880) were described by Luther Reed as "largely subjective and frequently Calvinistic in character" and largely ignored the church year. Benson characterized the hymns of the United Synod of the South's hymnal as containing "little or nothing to distinguish them from the hymn books of the surrounding Evangelical denominations." Only the General Council's *Church Book* (1868) escaped that kind of condemnation. The situation seemed ready for a new hymnal which might reclaim in its hymnody what the *Common Service* had reclaimed in liturgy.

The story of the development of the *Common Service Book and Hymnal* is told in great detail in Luther D. Reed, *The Lutheran Liturgy*, rev. ed., Fortress Press, 1947, pp. 182–204. Luther D. Reed's contribution and influence on the development of the *Common Service Book and Hymnal*—for which he served as chairman of the Editorial Committee, and Secretary of the Joint Committee and all its subcommittees—cannot be overestimated.

[3]That rule was: "The common consent of the pure Lutheran Liturgies of the Sixteenth Century, and when there is not an entire agreement among them, the consent of the largest number of those of greatest weight" (from the "Preface to the Common Service, 1888.")

[4]The hymnal contained 577 hymns with an appendix containing 19 alternate tunes.

[5]Approximately 20% of the hymns were from the German, the criterion of "literary merit" working to exclude many of the currently available translations that were found wanting. Not only German but Scandinavian hymnody as well was only meagerly represented. Henry E. Jacobs in an article "What Is a Real Lutheran Hymn," *Lutheran Church Review*, XLI (July 1922), 210–19, written to meet objections that the hymnal contained too small a proportion of hymns by Lutheran authors remarked: "The great bulk of this vast material [that is, translations into English of the German and Scandinavian hymnic heritage] was absolutely unusable. The difference in the structure of the languages, stands in the way of idiomatic translations." It remains ironic that a book which determined its liturgical formulations on the basis of the "common consent of the pure Lutheran Liturgies of the Sixteenth Century" should avoid so radically the Lutheran heritage of hymnody from that same time because the available translations were, in the opinion of its compilers, deficient in "literary merit."

[6]Jeremiah Franklin Ohl (1850–1941) was an American Lutheran pastor, hymnist, liturgist, and editor who was active in deaconess and prison reform work. He graduated from the Lutheran Theological Seminary in Philadelphia and served as pastor in Pennsylvania from 1874–93. He organized and directed the Lutheran Deaconess Motherhouse, Milwaukee, Wis., from 1893–98. He served as chairman of the music subcommittee for the *Common Service Book and Hymnal*, arranged the first setting of the service, and generally

supervised the music for the book. An article by Ohl, "The Liturgical Deterioration of the Seventeenth and Eighteenth Centuries" appears in the *Memoirs of the Lutheran Liturgical Association,* IV, 75–77. Two of Ohl's tunes survive in the *Service Book and Hymnal* (1958), nos. 507 (St. Chrysostom) and 520, second tune (Pilgrims).

7*The Choral Service Book.* ed. Harry G. Archer and Luther D. Reed. Philadelphia: The United Lutheran Publication House, 1901.

8This plainsong setting of the liturgy, included in the first edition, was deleted after 1919, Luther D. Reed remarking that it "proved in advance of the times."

22

American Lutheran Hymnal[1]

Not all Lutherans embraced the Common Service Book and Hymnal *of 1917. In 1921 a number of other groups—chief among them the Iowa, Buffalo, and Ohio Synods—explored the possibility of an inter-synodical hymnal, the result of their work appearing after nine years as the* American Lutheran Hymnal *(1930). That same year the Iowa, Buffalo, and Ohio Synods merged to form the American Lutheran Church.*

Music Edition, Compiled and Edited by an
Intersynodical Committee

Columbus, Ohio: The Lutheran Book Concern, 1930

Preface

The *American Lutheran Hymnal* is the result of a movement that originated in the Evangelical Lutheran Synod of Iowa and Other States.[2] In response to an invitation extended on behalf of that synodical body to all Lutheran synodical groups in America, representatives of eight synods,[3] some official and others unofficial, met in Chicago, May 3, 1921, and organized the Lutheran Intersynodical Hymnal Committee,[4] which has compiled and edited this book.

In 1928, after the Hymnal Committee had devoted much time and labor to a careful selection of hymns to be included in this hymnal and to a thorough revision of hymns from other languages as well as to the making of new translations when those hitherto used were not deemed satisfactory, a provisional text edition of limited size was printed and circulated, with a view to the solicitation of criticisms and suggestions. Conferences, synodical committees and individuals submitted constructive and helpful suggestions. These were given careful consideration. The Committee again revised its work, also eliminating 132 hymns, mostly translations, that had been printed in the provisional edition, and including 93 other hymns.

The Committee has aimed to provide a truly ecumenical selection of hymns. In choosing from the vast store of Christian lyrics, first, those hymns were selected that are found in all or the majority of English hymnals of our Church in America, and then such other hymns were added as were recommended in suggestions received by the Hymnal Committee, or, in its judgment, were thought necessary or desirable. Both those who prefer the ancient hymns and the texts of German and Scandinavian chorales, which have come to us in translations, as well as those who have greater liking for hymns originally written in the English language, will find that ample provision has been made to meet their need or preference. It is hoped, however, that full use will be made of the rich store of hymns from many sources, both ancient and modern, that is contained in the *American Lutheran Hymnal*.[5] It contains some hymns, hymn translations and tunes that appear in print for the first time. These are protected by copyright and may be used only by permission of the Lutheran Intersynodical Hymnal Committee.

As a rule, the original, rhythmical form of the German chorales has been used in the Music Edition of the Hymnal. In a number of instances, when a chorale tune has been used for several hymns, the non-rhythmical form has also been given. Thus the one form may be substituted for the other, if desired, by consulting the alphabetical index of Tunes. If it is desired to use another tune for a hymn than the one printed in the Music Edition of the Hymnal (in several instances two tunes have been given), a choice can easily be made by referring to the index of Metres.

Contributions of one kind or another to the contents of the Hymnal have come from many sources. It is impossible to name them, but the Hymnal Committee hereby expresses its gratitude to all who have aided and encouraged its efforts. The permission to use several copyrighted hymns and tunes is gratefully acknowledged and is indicated, in each instance, by a footnote. The careful revision of the Passion History of our

Lord Jesus Christ, made by Prof. G. C. Gast,[6] D. D., will be noted and appreciated by all who make use of it.

A courtesy deserving special mention is the permission, generously given by the Rev. F. H. Knubel,[7] D.D., L.L.D., President of the United Lutheran Church in America,[8] on its behalf to use the first musical setting for Holy Communion, Matins and Vespers of the *Common Service Book*.[9]

The undersigned wishes to record his personal gratitude to his esteemed colleague, the Rev. Wm. H. Lehmann,[10] D.D., for valuable assistance in the final editorial revision of the manuscript.

May the *American Lutheran Hymnal* help to glorify God and to edify His people! In order that it may do so, may those who use it in public worship and private devotion heed the admonition given singers in the choir schools of the early Christian Church, "Give diligence that thy heart believes what thy voice sings, and that thy life demonstrates what thy heart believes."

Emmanuel Poppen,[11] Chairman
Lutheran Intersynodical Hymnal Committee
September 1930

Notes

[1]Although this hymn book was used by most of the American Lutheran Church, it was not officially adopted as the church's hymnal until 1938.

[2]This synod, also known as the German Iowa Synod, was organized in 1854. It originally had ties with the Missouri Synod through the pastors that Wilhelm Loehe sent to America. These ties were broken because of doctrinal disagreements, thus giving cause for the formation of the Iowa Synod. It used many different hymnals before publishing its own *Wartburg Hymnal for Church, School, and Home* in 1918. In 1920, the Iowa Synod invited the Joint Synod of Ohio, which had for a while (1872–82) been a member of the Synodical Conference, for discussions on church union. In 1930, the two synods along with the Buffalo Synod formed the American Lutheran Church.

[3]Since 1918, the Iowa and Ohio Synods had altar and pulpit fellowship. Therefore, the Iowa Synod most likely invited the Ohio and Buffalo Synods along with other Lutheran bodies in this joint hymnal venture.

[4]According to minutes available, the Joint Synod of Ohio in 1928 approved the work of the Lutheran Intersynodical Hymnal Committee.

[5]The hymnal contains 651 hymns.

[6]G. C. Gast (b. 1888) was educated at Capital University (1908, B. A.;

1929, D. D.); Evangelical Lutheran Seminary (1911); University of Michigan (1919, M. A.); Augustana Seminary (1929, B. D.). He served Grace Lutheran Church, Hubbard, Ohio (1911–14). He was professor at St. Paul Luther Seminary (1914–17), becoming its president in 1917. In 1918 he became a professor at Evangelical Seminary, serving there until 1941, at which time he became a copy editor for Wartburg Press until 1960.

7F. H. Knubel (1870–1945) graduated from Gettysburg Lutheran Seminary, Gettysburg, Pennsylvania in 1895. He did some graduate work at the University of Leipzig (1895–96), was ordained in 1896, and founded and was pastor of Atonement Lutheran Church, New York City (1896–1923). He was the first president of the United Lutheran Church in America (1918–36).

8Organized in November, 1918, the United Lutheran Church in America was a merger of the General Synod, the General Council, and the United Synod of the South. Previously, all three bodies had worked together on the *Common Service Book* which appeared in 1917.

9The *Common Service Book*, the product of the three bodies that made up the U. L. C. A., was used by the Iowa Synod in many of its congregations while they were awaiting the publication of their new hymnal.

10Wm. H. Lehmann (b. 1868) was educated at Capital University (1886, B. A.; 1925, D. D.) and at the Evangelical Lutheran Seminary (1889). He served Lutheran parishes in Michigan, Indiana, Ohio, and Pennsylvania. He was president of the English District of the Synod of Ohio (1924–30). Later, he served as superintendant of Home Missions and the Lutheran Welfare Service of Northwest Ohio.

11Emmanuel Poppen (1874–1961) was educated at Capital University and the Evangelical Lutheran Seminary (1895; 1928, D. D.). He was editor of the *Kirchenzeitung* (1925–30), while also being a member of the Joint Merger Commission (1924–30), which formulated the American Lutheran Church, which he served as its second president (1937–50). In the *American Lutheran Hymnal*, appears the hymn tune he wrote for the text, "Jesus, Thou Joy of Loving Hearts" (#171).

23

The Lutheran Hymnal

The Lutheran Hymnal (1941) was the product of joint effort by the members of the Evangelical Lutheran Synodical Conference of North America which, at the time of the book's appearance, consisted of the Norwegian Synod of the American Evangelical Lutheran Church (the "Little Norwegian Synod"), the Joint Synod of Wisconsin, Minnesota, Michigan and Other States, the Slovak Evangelical Lutheran Synod, and—the largest of the group—The Lutheran Church—Missouri Synod. This book would continue to serve these groups—approximately one-third of American Lutherans— for over forty years, well beyond the dissolution of the Synodical Conference itself in 1967.

The Lutheran Hymnal

Authorized by the Synods Constituting
The Evangelical Lutheran Synodical Conference
of North America[1]

Concordia Publishing House, 1941

Preface

The Lutheran Hymnal is intended for use in church, school, and home. The committee entrusted with the task of compiling and editing has earnestly endeavored to produce a hymnal containing the best of the hymnological treasures of the Church, both as to texts and tunes, in accord with the highest standards of Christian worship. It is our sincere prayer that these treasures may be cherished by God's people wherever the English tongue is used in public or private worship. We have freely used whatever we found of value and, by way of acknowledgment, have carefully indicated all sources. In turn, we freely offer for the use of others all original contributions or translations made by the committee as such or by its individual members.

"Unto Him that loved us and washed us from our sins in His own blood and hath made us kings and priests unto God and His Father: to Him be glory and dominion forever and ever! Amen."

The Intersynodical Committee On Hymnology and Liturgies For the Ev. Luth. Synodical Conference of North America

The Preface to The Handbook to the Lutheran Hymnal *(compiled by W. G. Polack, St. Louis: Concordia Publishing House, 1942) reproduced below includes much information concerning the background and development of The Lutheran Hymnal.*

Preface

The Lutheran Hymnal has its antecedents in earlier English hymn collections used by the respective synods of the Synodical Conference.

The Norwegian Synod of the American Evangelical Lutheran Church has been using the *Lutheran Hymnary* of 1913, originally published by authority of the Norwegian Evangelical Lutheran Synod, the Hauge Evangelical Lutheran Synod, and the United Norwegian Lutheran Church of America.

The Slovak Evangelical Lutheran Synod of the United States of America has been using the *Evangelical Lutheran Hymn-book* of 1912, published by the Evangelical Lutheran Synod of Missouri, Ohio, and Other States.

The Joint Synod of Wisconsin, Minnesota, Michigan, and Other States published its first English hymnbook in 1910. It was a text edition, containing 115 hymns, and was entitled *Church Hymnal*. This was followed in 1920 by its *Book of Hymns*, with tunes, containing 320 hymns. The chief editors were the Revs. O. Hagedorn and H. K. Moussa. The collection was based largely on the *Evangelical Lutheran Hymn-book* of

1912.

The English hymnals used by individual congregations of the Evangelical Lutheran Synod of Missouri, Ohio, and Other States antedate any official hymnals published by that body. Some congregations used the *Hymn-book for Use of Ev. Luth. Schools and Congregations*, published by the Lutheran Publishing House, Decorah, Ia., 1879, containing translations by Prof. August Crull. Others used the hymnal published by Concordia Publishing House very likely in 1888. It was a small collection of hymns, entitled *Hymns of the Ev. Luth Church for the Use of English Lutheran Missions*. It contained 33 hymns, with the music for the soprano voice only placed above the hymns. This collection also contained translations by Prof. August Crull. It passed through many printings until it was superseded either by the "Grey Hymnal" or by the "Baltimore Hymnal." Other congregations, for a time at least, used hymnals published by the Joint Synod of Ohio, the General Council, and the Tennessee Synod.

The English Lutheran Conference of Missouri, the forerunner of the English Evangelical Lutheran Synod of Missouri and Other States, now the English District of the Evangelical Lutheran Synod of Missouri, Ohio, and Other States, published its own hymnal. This hymnal had been prepared by Prof. August Crull of Concordia College, Fort Wayne, Ind., and was presented by him to the Conference at its meeting in 1888. It was published under the title *Evangelical Lutheran Hymn-book*, at Baltimore, 1889, by the Lutheran Publication Board, for the Conference. It was a text edition only and contained 400 hymns, the three ecumenical creeds of Christendom, the Augsburg Confession, and an order for morning service and evening service which had been prepared by a committee elected by the Conference for that purpose. This was commonly known as the "Baltimore Hymnal." A new edition of this hymnal was ordered by the Conference when it constituted itself as a synod in 1891. Fifty hymns were added, and the Common Service, Matins, and Vespers were included after permission had been received from the General Synod, the General Council, and the United Synod of the South, a joint committee of these bodies having prepared the orders. This new edition, also published at Baltimore, appeared in 1892. It also was a text edition only. Later this hymnal was published at Pittsburgh and was thereafter known as the "Pittsburgh

Hymnal." An edition was also published at Chicago in 1895. It contained, besides the Common Service, Matins, and Vespers, other liturgical material and a selection of psalms. An edition of this hymnal, in which the liturgical section was abridged, appeared in 1905.

In the same year Concordia Publishing House published the so-called "Grey Hymnal," edited by Prof. F. Bente of Concordia Seminary, St. Louis. It was entitled *Hymnal for Evangelical Lutheran Missions* and contained the text of 199 hymns, without music, three doxologies, no order of service, except for Communion, and a list of antiphons or versicles.

In the meantime the English Evangelical Lutheran Synod of Missouri, Ohio, and Other States had appointed a Tune-book Committee, composed in 1891 of the Revs. W. Dallmann, Theo. Huegli, A. S. Bartholomew, and Oscar Kaiser, which was to prepare an edition of its *Evangelical Lutheran Hymn-book* with tunes. This committee in 1897 included the Revs. W. Dallmann, C. C. Morhart, B. H. Hemmeter,[2] Oscar Kaiser, Adam Detzer, and W. P. Sachs.

The work proceeded slowly. Ultimately Teachers Herman Ilse and H. A. Polack were appointed as a special committee on the music of it. When in 1911, at St. Louis, the English Evangelical Lutheran Synod of Missouri became the English District of the Evangelical Lutheran Synod of Missouri, Ohio, and Other States, the *Evangelical Lutheran Hymn-book*, which was ready for publication, was presented to Synod. It appeared in the spring of 1912 and became the official English hymnal of Synod. It contained a liturgical section of 112 pages, 567 hymns, 8 chants, and 17 doxologies.

When the Delegate Convention of the Evangelical Lutheran Synod of Missouri, Ohio, and Other States, in triennial assembly at River Forest, Ill., in 1929, authorized the revision of the *Evangelical Lutheran Hymn-book* of 1912, it was stipulated that the sister synods of the Synodical Conference of North America be requested to cooperate in order that the final result might be a common English hymnal for that federation. Dr. F. Pfotenhauer, President of the Missouri Synod, appointed the Committee on English Hymnology and Liturgics for this group, consisting of the following members: The Rev. Prof. W. G. Polack, Chairman, the Rev. Prof. L. Fuerbringer, D. D., the Rev. O. Kaiser, the Rev. Prof. L. Blankenbuehler, and Mr. B. Schumacher. This committee held its organization meeting at St.

Louis, Mo., Nov. 20, 1929, and tentatively outlined its program.

In the meantime the sister synods of the Synodical Conference, through their respective presidents, had reacted favorably to the suggested plan of cooperation and on Jan. 3, 1930, the Intersynodical Committee on Hymnology and Liturgics was organized in Milwaukee, Wis., with the Rev. Prof. W. G. Polack as Chairman and Mr. B. Schumacher[3] as Secretary. In addition to the representatives of the Missouri Synod mentioned above, the committee included the following representatives: The Rev. Prof. J. Meyer and the Rev. O. Hagedorn (Joint Synod of Wisconsin); the Revs. N. A. Madson and C. Anderson (Norwegian Synod); the Rev. J. Pelikan (Slovak Synod). The latter was present at the second meeting, April, 1930.

In 1931 Dr. L. Fuerbringer tendered his resignation, owing to his increased duties as President of Concordia Seminary, St. Louis, and was made honorary member of the committee. The Rev. Wm. Moll of Fort Wayne was later appointed by Pres. F. Pfotenhauer to take his place. The Rev. O. Hagedorn was removed from the committee by death, and the Rev. Arthur Voss was appointed in his place in 1932. In 1933 the Rev. A. Harstad was appointed to the committee as a third representative of the Norwegian Synod. In 1934 the Rev. Wm. Moll resigned from the committee on account of failing health, and the Rev. O. H. Schmidt was appointed in his place. When the Rev. J. Pelikan resigned in 1938, The Revs. J. Bajus and J. Kucharik were appointed to represent the Slovak Synod. When death took the Rev. Prof. A. Zich from the committee, the Rev. W. J. Schaefer, who had been active for years as a subcommittee member, was appointed to succeed him.

The individuals who assisted in the work, as members of subcommittees, for longer or shorter periods, are the following: The Revs. W. M. Czamanske, W. Lochner, W. Burhop, K. Ehlers, J. H. Deckmann, C. M. Waller, C. Hoffmann, C. Bergen, G. W. Fischer; the Rev. Profs. W. Schaller, W. Buszin, R. W. Heintze, M. Lochner; Profs. K. Haase, E. Backer; The Rev. Drs. J. H. Ott, P. E. Kretzmann, A. W. Wismar, S. C. Ylvisaker.[4]

In its plan of work the committee proceeded to study, through subcommittees, the hymns (a) of English and American origin (not by Lutheran authors); (b) of German origin; (c) of Scandinavian origin; (d) of American Lutheran origin; (e) of ancient and medieval origin; (f) the music of the hymns; and (g) the liturgy.

These following general guiding principles were accepted.

1. Hymns:
    a. They must be of intrinsic value as to content;
    b. They must be distinctively Christian.
2. Translations:
    a. They must be of good form;
    b. They must be in idiomatic English.
3. Tunes
    a. They must be suited to the text;
    b. They must be good church music. (Exceptions may be made in such cases in which texts and tunes are so wedded as to be practically inseparable.)

As to the liturgical section of *The Lutheran Hymnal*, the committee held it to be within the scope of its work to make no changes in the liturgies as such but to simplify the rubrics as much as possible, to correct any discrepancies, to supply the most necessary general rubrics, to add the graduals for the Sundays, feasts, and festivals in the church-year, to provide the introits, graduals, collects, etc., for the minor festivals, etc. Additional psalms were added and all tables of lessons, etc., were carefully checked. All musical settings for the responses and chants were likewise revised.

While the committee was engaged in its task, it received many suggestions from members in all parts of the Synodical Conference and made periodical reports in the *Lutheran Witness* as follows: Jan. 16, 1934; March 27, 1934; Nov. 5, 1935; Oct. 20, 1936, and Nov. 9. 1937; a report in pamphlet form in the spring of 1938, a report to the respective synods in 1938, and a final comprehensive report, in pamphlet form, May 1, 1939. After having carefully considered all criticisms and suggestions that were submitted to the committee on the basis of these reports, and after having then reviewed once more its entire work of over ten years, the committee finally turned over the manuscript to Concordia Publishing House, St. Louis, Mo., in April 1940. This publication house had undertaken the work of producing the hymnal for the synods directly interested. The suggestions of the committee as to the style of type, the arrangement of the pages, the paper, the binding, etc., were painstakingly followed by Concordia Publishing House, which had also previously given its full cooperation to the committee in various ways.

The committee had planned to include among the indexes of *The Lutheran Hymnal* an index of Bible texts, of authors and composers, of original first lines, and of topics. However, in order not to bulk the hymnal too much, the committee requested the chairman to include these indexes in the *Handbook to the Lutheran Hymnal*.

Notes

[1]These were the Norwegian Synod of the American Evangelical Lutheran Church, the Slovak Evangelical Lutheran Synod of the United States of America, the Joint Synod of Wisconsin, Minnesota, Michigan, and Other States, and the Evangelical Lutheran Synod of Missouri, Ohio, and Other States.

[2]This should be H. B. Hemmeter.

[3]Bernard Schumacher, a Lutheran parochial school teacher from Milwaukee, Wisconsin, was a prominent Lutheran musician of his day. It is generally thought that he was responsible for the harmonizations in *The Lutheran Hymnal*.

[4]From this listing, those possessing particular musical expertise included: Carl Bergen, Walter Buszin, Martin Lochner, Karl Haase, Emil Backer, and Adolph W. Wismar.

24

Service Book and Hymnal of the Lutheran Church in America

The Service Book and Hymnal *(1958) was the result of joint work by the United Lutheran Church in America and a cluster of smaller, independent church bodies with Danish, Swedish, German, Norwegian, and Finnish backgrounds. Begun in 1945, the book appeared thirteen years later, the names most prominently associated with the work being Luther D. Reed and E. E. Ryden. By the early 1960s the eight cooperating Lutheran bodies had merged into two larger groups: The American Lutheran Church, formed in 1960, and the Lutheran Church in America, formed in 1962. The* Service Book and Hymnal *was to serve approximately two-thirds of American Lutheranism for the next twenty years, the remaining one-third utilizing* The Lutheran Hymnal.

Service Book and Hymnal of the Lutheran Church in America

Authorized by the Churches cooperating in The Commission on the Liturgy and The Commission on the Hymnal

Copyright 1958 by The American Evangelical Lutheran Church, The American Lutheran Church, The Augustana Evangelical Lutheran Church, The Evangelical Lutheran Church, The Finnish Evangelical Lutheran Church in America, The Lutheran Free Church, The United Evangelical Lutheran Church, The United Lutheran Church in America

Introduction to the Common Hymnal

The birth of Jesus was announced in song, and the last act of worship of our Lord and his Disciples was the singing of a hymn. Sacred song, rooted in the Hebrew tradition, occupied from the first a preeminent position in Christian worship. The earliest hymns were psalms and canticles. Initially the people sang them, though by the fourth century in the East, and by the seventh in the West, they had become part of the liturgy and a matter for the clergy and the choirs. Not again until the time of the Reformation was the hymn restored to the people as their rightful heritage in worship.

In 1524, Luther published the *Achtliederbuch,* which led the way for an outburst of evangelical hymnody in the countries of Northern and Central Europe. Next there came a new type of music, the chorale, based sometimes on plainsong, sometimes on secular melodies. The hymn was incorporated into the services of the Church and once more was congregational. In sharp contrast, the Reformed churches employed only the Psalter, often crudely paraphrased, and it was not until the eighteenth century that the hymn made its way in the English-speaking world.

When Lutherans came to the New World, they brought with them the hymnals of their homelands, but as their descendants grew up in an English-speaking environment, English Lutheran hymnals began to appear. Attempts were made to translate hymns of the Lutheran heritage and to incorporate the finest English hymns. Each Lutheran body used its own hymnal, but there was a growing feeling that there was a body of common hymnody sufficient to permit the preparation of a common hymnal. In 1944, the United Lutheran Church directed its Common Service Book Committee (which had been engaged for four years in studies envisaging the revision of its own hymnal) "to seek the fullest possible cooperation with other Lutheran bodies in the hope of producing a Common Lutheran Hymnal in America."[1] Upon the subsequent invitation, representatives of the American Lutheran Church, the Augustana Lutheran Church, the Evangelical Lutheran Church, and the United Lutheran Church, met in Pittsburgh, Pa., June, 1945, to inaugurate this work.[2]

The Commission on a Common Hymnal followed these basic principles: The Common Hymnal must be a new work, not simply a conflation of the existing hymnals; it must contain only good hymns providing, as a companion to the liturgy, for the full round of the Christian Year and the Christian Life; the hymns should be devotional rather than didactic or homiletical,[3] and their direction Godward, not manward; the hymnal must be ecumenical in character, expressing the continuity and catholicity of the life of the Church; the final criterion is not Lutheran authorship, but agreement with the teachings of the Word of God; the hymnal must have the highest standards of literary excellence, and each hymn, being an act of worship, should be exalted in language, noble in thought, and reverent in feeling.

One of the most difficult problems was the application of this final principle, especially to hymns of our own heritage where pressure was great for their inclusion. Inferior translations have been accepted in the past because of the affection felt for the original, or because of a majestic chorale tune with which the original text was associated. What is often forgotten, or perhaps charitably overlooked, is the fact that a translation seldom succeeds in recreating either the poetic beauty or depth of message of the original.[4] The Commission has found it necessary to edit and, in some cases, re–translate, some of these hymns. It hopes that it has thus enriched the hymnal by many hymns from sources largely unknown in the New World, and that some of these may eventually become part of the ecumenical treasury of Christian hymnody.

In addition to hymns of Lutheran provenance, and the best of the ancient Greek and Latin hymns, nearly two-thirds of the hymns are of English and American authorship. Many of them have been in our hymnals for years, and the nearly 80 of American authorship will correct a weakness common to our hymnals. A few original hymns appear here for the first time. In general, the Commission has respected the original texts of the authors, though in some cases, generally accepted alterations have been adopted. Where this has been done, "a." (altered) follows the author's name.

As far as possible, hymns have been placed where they will be of the greatest general use, and only a minimum appear under the more restrictive rubrics of the Church Year. Extensive cross-references at the end of each section of the hymnal, and indexes at the end of the book, afford an increased selection of hymns for particular occasions.

The music, like the texts, is ecumenical. The characteristic Lutheran form, the chorale, is well-represented in rhythmic, isometric and Bach arrangements. An increased number of plainsong melodies on the other hand, and some Gospel hymns on the other, will provide for a wide variety of taste among our people. About two hundred fifty hymns have tunes of English origin, including both the standard tunes of the nineteenth century and some by contemporary composers. Psalm tunes from English, Scottish, Swiss and French sources appear, as well as eight Welsh tunes and a number of French tunes based on plainsong. Carols and more than thirty folksongs, largely from North European sources, add much new and interesting music. American composers are well represented, some by tunes which appear here for the first time.

The Commission has tried not to disturb the association of certain hymns with certain tunes, except in instances where the traditional tune has become worn by usage. In such cases a second tune has been provided in the hope of lending new freshness to the text, and often, where a new tune appears, a cross-reference indicates where the older tune may be located. The pitch of many of the hymns has been lowered to encourage congregational singing by men as well as women. Solid notes have usually been employed in notation, except in the case of psalm tunes, some chorales and modern compositions of grave character. Eighth notes have been used in plainsong. For every hymn, a direction indicates the mood and tempo of the tune, and organists and choirmasters should note these suggestions carefully. Amen has not been provided for hymns which are didactic, hortatory, narrative or contemplative, but it appears, properly, at the conclusion of hymns which end in prayer or praise. Double bars are employed at the end of musical rather than textual phrases.

The Commission expresses its appreciation to all who have granted permission for the use of copyrighted material, and hopes that all such material has been properly credited. It also records, with a deep sense of sorrow and loss, the death of five of its members since the inception of its work: the Rev. Paul Zeller Strodach, D.D., of the United Lutheran Church; the Rev. C. A. Wendell, D.D., Litt.D., and the Rev. Carl J. Sodergren, D.D., both of the Augustana Lutheran Church; and the Rev.

Albert Jagnow, PhD., and the Rev. Leonard O. Barry, both of the American Lutheran Church. All of them made important contributions and it is to be regretted that they did not live to see the completion of this work.

Since 1945, four additional bodies of Lutherans have become associated in this project: the Lutheran Free Church, The United Evangelical Lutheran Church, the Finnish Evangelical Lutheran Church, and the American Evangelical Lutheran Church. This assures the use of the Common Hymnal by more than two-thirds of the Lutherans in the United States and Canada. After the appearance of the Common Liturgy and Hymnal, a permanent Commission on the Liturgy and Hymnal, will come into being and will have full jurisdiction over this book, other and subsequent editions and companion volumes.

The Lutheran Churches in America are in process of becoming the Lutheran Church in America. We share the rich endowments of a common faith, a common history, a common heritage of liturgy and hymnody, and the recognition of a common mission and destiny in the New World. This book will contribute to the unity of our Church and to the advent of the day when Henry Melchior Muhlenberg's vision of "one Church and one book" will become a reality.[3] May God accept the worship this volume brings. To his glory we dedicate the *Service Book and Hymnal* with the prayer that he may bless it and use it as an instrument of his grace and power for the advancement of his kingdom.

Notes

[1]The Lutheran Church-Missouri Synod was among the churches that had been invited, but President Behnken replied to Dr. Reed: "Our Synod recently published a new hymnal. It was a joint effort with the constituent members of the Synodical Conference. The new hymnal contains the liturgy which is now used quite extensively in our circles and is being introduced in many places where very little liturgy formerly was in use. Our Synod would not be interested now in effecting another change." Portions of this correspondence as well as Luther Reed's reply is given in Luther D. Reed, *The Lutheran Liturgy*. rev. ed., Fortress Press, 1947, pp. 208–09. The detailed history of the development of the *Service Book and Hymnal* is given in *The Lutheran Liturgy*, pp. 205 ff.

[2]The Joint Commission on the Hymnal was organized at First English Lutheran Church in Pittsburgh, Pa., on June 23, 1945. At a subsequent meeting Luther D. Reed was elected permanent chairman and E. E. Ryden, secretary.

The *Service Book and Hymnal* is generally considered to be the culminating achievement of Reed and those who shared his vision of worship of beauty, dignity, and truly Lutheran. Reed had served for 34 years as professor of liturgics and church art at Lutheran Theological Seminary in Philadelphia, serving as president of the seminary from 1938–45.

3The goal that hymns should be "devotional rather than didactic or homiletical" was clearly at variance with the understanding of the 16th century. Ulrich Leopold points out that Luther's hymns "were meant not to create a mood, but *to convey a message* [emphasis mine]. They were a confession of faith, not of personal feelings.... They present their subject vidly and dramatically, but without the benefit of ornate language and other poetic refinements" (LW 53:197). Using the artistic canons of 19th-century Romanticism as a basis for judging the Lutheran hymnody of the 16th century—"beautifully polished phrases and dance or march rhythms to create a certain modd and to give an ornate expression to personal religious feelings"(Ibid.)—it is understandable why the Lutheran chorale was so poorly represented in both the *Serivce Book and Hymnal* and the earlier *Common Service Book and Hymnal*.

4The application of the standard of "literary excellence" and the corollary concern of the Comission that "a translation seldom succeeds in recreating either the poetic beauty or depth of message of the original" worked to exclude the bulk of 16th-century Lutheran hymnody from the *Service Book and Hymnal*. As with the *Common Service Book and Hymnal* some 40 years earlier—these same concerns—undoubtedly promulgated by Luther D. Reed who was the guiding force in both of these publications—had been applied with similar results.

5Only a few years following the publication of the *Service Book and Hymnal* in 1958, the participating bodies had merged into two larger bodies forming The American Lutheran Church (1960) and the Lutheran Church in America (1962).

25

Worship Supplement.[1]

Worship Supplement (1969), which had its origin in the latter 1950s, was intended to function as a supplement to The Lutheran Hymnal *in the years before a new revised worship resource could be prepared. While its use in congregations was not widespread, it was an important publication which helped shape—both in its hymnody and in its liturgical material—the direction of future Lutheran hymnals. The names most prominently associated with this publication are Paul Bunjes and Richard Hillert.*

Worship Supplement

Authorized by the Commission on Worship, The Lutheran Church—Missouri Synod and Synod of Evangelical Lutheran Churches. Concordia Publishing House, St. Louis. 1969

Foreword to the Tune-Text Edition

More than a generation has passed since *The Lutheran Hymnal* first appeared in 1941. The intervening years have brought many changes in Christian living that have led to new worship needs. New concerns for social structures, colleges, armed forces, missions, the inner city, and racially or culturally conscious groups have raised a need for updating liturgical and hymnodic materials both as to language and form.

When this need first began to be felt, a thorough revision of *The Lutheran Hymnal* was planned and begun. The project was abandoned several years ago in favor of a program designed to lead to an eventual all-Lutheran hymnal in English.[2] The present *Worship Supplement* was meanwhile chosen to supply the worship needs of the Church until the proposed long-range project could produce a more permanent hymnal.[3] It was adopted as a convenient stage in the development of new types and forms of worship materials which, by meeting the demands of changing times and situations, might serve also as a modern experiment in applying timeless truths to timely needs, an attempt to give voice to the cries and joys of today's Christian by means of contemporary creations.

Much of the language of the liturgies and the hymns was found to be in need of revision to make it meaningful to the man of today. In some liturgical texts the Commission on Worship produced its own revised versions (Gloria, Te Deum), in others it adopted those suggested by the Committee on Common Liturgical Texts (Our Father, Apostolic Creed, Nicene Creed).

The Commission was also interested in restoring appropriate materials that had fallen into disuse and in preparing or adapting new materials for today. Additional revised offertories, prayers, collects, and other historic forms are provided. Several new services are included. Among the latter are two orders for Holy Communion designed for special use and three experimental services of prayer and preaching. Other new items include the Old Testament Lesson, an expanded Kyrie, the singing of the Offertory as the offerings are brought forward, congregational responses and petitions in the Intercessions, and the Prayer of Thanksgiving.[4]

The Commission wishes to supply examples of traditional hymns revised for modern use and new hymns relevant to the life of the Christian in the world today.

Worship Supplement is issued in two books: one, a tune-text edition for the orders of service and the hymns; the other, a keyboard edition containing the accompaniments. All melodies have been set in a comfortable singing range. The most convenient notation, generally the quarter note, has been used. Bar lines are used when they help and are suppressed when they hinder the understanding of the rhythmic layout of the tune.

The melodies for the orders of service are entirely new; no historic compositions, fragments of the same, or chants have been retained. These tunes move about in a comfortable middle range. In the short responses no meters are indicated, and only short and long notes (quarters and halves) are used; their precise time values are derived from the text.

The longer compositions (for example, "Lord, Have Mercy," "Holy, Holy, Holy," and "Lamb of God") are nonmetrical yet rhythmic, for they seek to present the text as naturally as possible. But in each composition the generative musical material has been held to a minimum to facilitate learning and to promote unity. The music of the liturgy is the work of Paul Bunjes and Richard Hillert both members of the Music Committee of the Commission on worship.[5]

For the 93 hymn texts, 87 tunes were assembled (six tunes serve two hymns each), of which 10 are original melodies introduced into a service book for the first time. Sources of texts and tunes are given with the individual hymns. The numbering of the hymns begins at 701 for convenient reference.

It is the hope of the Commission that the worship materials presented in this booklet may be a God-pleasing addition to existing hymnals, serve the present needs of the Church, and be a helpful contribution to service books of the future. Throughout its work of expanding the Church's worship resources, the Commission made every effort to preserve the Church's dedication to true worship and Biblical doctrine.

"Something must be dared in the name of Christ."—Martin Luther (first order of service, 1523).

Commission on Worship

Preface to the Accompaniment Edition

Worship Supplement is issued in two books: one, a tune-text edition for the use of the worshiper; the other, the present Accompaniment Edition.

Tune-Text Edition

In this *Supplement* the melodies of the plainsong tunes, the hymns, and the chorales have been set in a comfortable singing range for the worshiper. A generally black notation in quarter notes has been adopted for the hymns and chorales because it seems more familiar to the musical amateur than either an eighth-note or a white-note representation; only in rare and compelling instances has this policy been relaxed to admit the latter conditions.

The bar lines, which help to visualize the rhythmic disposition of the melodies, have all been reappraised in the light of each hymn's time of origin, and a grid has been cast that seeks to reveal the inherent rhythmic layout and metric organization of the tune. In many instances where a full-scale grid would appear overly contrived, the bar line has been suppressed.

The melodies for the orders of service are entirely new; no historical compositions, fragments of the same, or chants have been retained. The order of the Holy Eucharist lies generally around an F-A tonal center, the Offices around an E-G tonal center. The traditional reciting tone—frequently uncontrollable—has been suppressed in all pieces that require group participation without rehearsal. The short verses and responses are not metered: two note values are used to show "short" and "long," the quarter and the half note; their precise time values must be derived from the associated text. In the compositions ("Lord, Have Mercy," "Glory to God," "What Shall I Render," "Holy, Holy, Holy," "Lamb of God," "O Come, Let Us Sing," "We Praise You," "Blessed Be the Lord," and "My Soul Magnifies the Lord") the unit value is the quarter note, and this serves as the measure for all others. Unmetrical, yet rhythmic, the compositions seek to declaim the text in as natural, intelligible, and effective a manner as a measured representation will allow.

The compositions in the order of the Holy Eucharist are organized in a thematic scheme to produce an overall arch form: the thematic material of "Lord, Have Mercy" finds recall in "Lamb of God"; the themes of "Glory to God" find reapplication in "Holy, Holy, Holy." Again, in the Offices certain of the compositions are cut from the same cloth: the thematic material of "Blessed Be the Lord" serves again to generate "My Soul Magnifies the Lord." Within each composition, however, the generative musical material has been held to a minimum to insure greater unity and to present only a small amount of material for the worshiper to learn and assimilate.

Accompaniment Edition—Orders of Service

The settings for the orders of service employ generally a thin two- to three-part fabric for the chants of the officiant and a four–part texture (with occasional excursions into three parts) for the chants of the worshipers. Concise organ intonations should be used only where required to set a pitch level; these should be derived from the opening notes of the chant as shown in several instances.

In the short verses and responses care should be exercised to accompany the chant in such a way that the preeminence of the text declamation is not violated nor even disturbed. In the compositions (for example, "Glory to God" and "Holy, Holy, Holy") a well-defined pace should be set and consistently held, the quarter note serving as the unit of measure; in these the music exhibits a recognizable life of its own—albeit carefully fitted to the rhythm of the text—and seeks a legitimate rhythmic course of its own.

Registrations for the service music should generally be on the sparse side for the short verses and responses, the former without pedal, the latter, with or without, as the situation may require. In the compositions the substance of the registration should be diligently searched for in the musical content of the same, the meaning of the text, the complement of singers, and the like. Depending on the organization of the antiphonal compositions ("Glory to God," "O Come, Let Us Sing," "We Praise You," "Blessed Be the Lord," and "My Soul Magnifies the Lord"), two divisions of the organ may well be used in alternation, or the player may alternate between sections with and without pedal, and the like. Climactic moments ("Hosanna in the highest") require a sturdy and tonally rich support from the organ if they are to incite the worshipers to exult; other portions may require a meditative or reflective mood or one of resignation; all such should find appropriate and fitting expression in the registrations and manner of performance on the organ.

In a congregation that is unfamiliar with the musical expression of these orders of service, it is advisable to introduce the music with the congregations's foreknowledge and to make appropriate preparations in the choir, among the children of the school, etc., so that a reasonable respectable transition can be effected in public worship from the old to the new. In some instances it may be a distinct advantage to divide the service into four or five portions and to introduce one new portion at a time, each one awaiting the assimilation of its preceding segment before its own introduction.

Accompaniment Edition—Hymns

In most instances, two harmonizations are provided for each hymn, the first in a simple style for piano or organ without pedal or with optional pedal, the second in an idiomatic polyphonic texture for organ with obligatory pedal. Among the hymns, the simple keyboard accompaniment—which is always printed first—is especially recommended to players of limited skill, such as have small hands, such as must play the accompaniments on instruments without pedal keys or with insufficient pedal keys, or such as are not adequately skillful in pedal technique. The harmonizations have been freshly and carefully prepared or, in some instances, selected from the existing repertoire to meet these conditions in an effective way without relinquishing musical quality; they are for this reason to be regarded not as second rate but rather as on a par in their musical quality with the more difficult organ settings.

The second settings are written in the distinctive idiom and technique of the organ. Because of their somewhat polyphonic fabric, they presuppose skillful players and require meticulous performance. Skillful players may choose to use both settings when accompanying on the organ, using the second setting as the basic one for the hymn but substituting the simpler keyboard setting for one or more interior stanzas as the thought or mood of the text may suggest, thereby enriching and diversifying the musical content of a hymn or chorale with many stanzas.

For the accompaniment of the congregation a plenum registration of appropriate caliber should be drawn: Principal voices on various pitch levels (Principal 8', Octave 4', Rauschquinte 2-2/3' and 2', Mixture) or on relatively superior levels of registration and non-Principals on the inferior levels (Gedackt 8', Octave 4', Nasat 2-2/3', Octave 2'). In all cases a well-defined and substantial pedal registration should be drawn to support the texture adequately and convincingly and to help carry the worshipers effectively.

The tempos adopted for the hymns will be influenced by many factors (size of the worshiping congregation, season of the year, liturgical season or occasion, time of day, character of the hymn, length of the phrases, etc.) but should never be torpid on the one hand or hasty on the other. A good pace, rhythmically well defined and consistently maintained, will do much to insure hearty particiation by the worshipers. Silent singing by the organist is helpful in keeping him alert and sensitive to the establishment and maintenance of a tight rhythm and an appropriate pace.

The work of preparing the musical content of the *Supplement* fell to the members of the Music Committee of the Commission on Worship: Theodore Beck, Jan Bender, Paul Bunjes (chairman), Richard Hillert, Edward Klammer, Herbert Nuechterlein, and Carl Schalk.[6] Individual contributions (compositions or settings) are gratefully acknowledged and identified by initials.

Commission on Worship

Notes

[1]This official supplement to *The Lutheran Hymnal* of 1941 was published in two editions: a tune-text edition for the worshiper, and an accompaniment edition for the organist. The prefatory remarks to both editions contain valuable information as to the intent and design of these materials.

[2]The desire for a revision of *The Lutheran Hymnal* of 1941 is reflected in the official proceedings of The Lutheran Church— Missouri Synod throughout the later 1950s and early 1960s. In 1965 in its convention in Detroit, Mich., the LCMS abandoned its work on a unilateral revision of *The Lutheran Hymnal* and determined to invite all interested Lutheran church bodies to begin work on the joint preparation of worship materials leading to a book of liturgies and hymns which could be used by all.

[3]The "more permanent hymnal" was the *Lutheran Book of Worship* published in 1978, nine years after the publication of *Worship Supplement*.

[4]The "expanded Kyrie" in slightly different form was already used in the *Service Book and Hymnal* of 1958 as was the Prayer of Thanksgiving. *Worship Supplement* offered three alternative Prayers of Thanksgiving.

[5]The work of these two men in fashioning a musical liturgy which has a distinct unity is remarkable. This work is of special interest since Richard Hillert later became the music editor of the *Lutheran Book of Worship* (1978) and contributed the first setting of the Holy Communion to that volume, and Paul Bunjes later became the music editor of *Lutheran Worship* (1982). At that time both men were on the faculty of Concordia Teachers College, River Forest, Ill.

[6]At the time of the preparation of these materials, Theodore Beck was a member of the faculty at Concordia Teachers College, Seward, Neb.; Jan Bender was teaching at Wittenberg University, Springfield, Ohio; Herbert Nuechterlein taught at Concordia Senior College, Ft. Wayne, Ind.; Edward

Klammer was head of the music department at Concordia Publishing House, St. Louis, Mo.; and Paul Bunjes, Richard Hillert, and Carl Schalk were teaching at Concordia Teachers College, River Forest, IL

26

Lutheran Book of Worship[1]

By the early 1960s two hymnals were serving American Lutheranism: the Service Book and Hymnal *(1958) used by approximately two-thirds of Lutheran congregations, and* The Lutheran Hymnal *(1941), used by the remaining third. In 1965 the Lutheran Church—Missouri Synod invited all other Lutheran to join together in the preparation of a single book to serve all American Lutherans. After twelve years the* Lutheran Book of Worship *(1978) appeared, the joint work of the Lutheran Church in America, The American Lutheran Church, The Evangelical Lutheran Church of Canada, and The Lutheran Church—Missouri Synod. Concerns by some within The Lutheran Church—Missouri Synod led to the decision in 1979 by that church body to publish a "revised edition" of* Lutheran Book of Worship, *which appeared four years later as* Lutheran Worship *(1982). In 1988 the Lutheran Church in America and The American Lutheran Church merged to form the Evangelical Lutheran Church in America.*

Lutheran Book of Worship

Prepared by the churches participating
in the Inter-Lutheran Commission on Worship:
Lutheran Church in America
The American Lutheran Church,
The Evangelical Lutheran Church of Canada
The Lutheran Church—Missouri Synod

Published by Augsburg Publishing House,
Minneapolis, Board of Publication, Lutheran Church
in America, Philadelphia, 1978

Corporate worship expresses the unity of the people of God

and their continuity with Christians across the ages. In the liturgical tradition are the gestures, songs, and words by which Christians have identified themselves and each other. The Lutheran Confessions set our liturgical life within that mainstream of Christian worship: "We do not abolish the Mass but religiously keep and defend it. . . We keep traditional liturgical forms" (*Apology to the Ausburg Confession*, 24).

All that is edifying and authentic in the life of the Church of every time and every place is affirmed. Only that which is contrary to the Gospel is rejected. Empowered by the Holy Spirit, the reformers led the people of God across the barrier between Latin and the vernaculars of the West, just as the barrier between Greek and Latin had been crossed centuries earlier. The transition in language contributed to a new outpouring in the arts of worship, notably in hymns and other music.

The flowering of popular hymnody is the greatest of the artistic contributions of the Lutheran churches. Not since the early years of the Latin Church had there been such an outpouring by hymnists and composers. The Reformation hymn provided, once again, an open channel through which the people's thanks and praise for the Gospel could flow. And, all the while, it sang that Gospel into their hearts. The elemental merging of tune and text resulted in a rugged, vital song which, still today, inspires an ever-growing choral and instrumental literature. The key to the particularity of Lutheran worship is the Lutheran love of hymns.

Europeans carried out the task of reforming the liturgy and returning it to the language of the people by territories. A large number of Lutheran church liturgies in the languages of Germany, Scandinavia, central Europe, and the Baltic countries was the result. Lutherans who emigrated to North America took with them their hymnals and service books; the traditions were transplanted, but almost immediately the emigrants began to respond to the new situation and the new land.

The worship life of Lutherans in North America has been enriched by this variegated heritage and by the transition to the English language. Worshiping in English led to the use of English hymns and the majestic language of the Authorized Version of the Bible and the *Book of Common Prayer*.

Common use of English also stimulated the quest for liturgical uniformity. The foundation was laid in 1748 by the

German liturgy of Henry Melchior Muhlenberg. It exhibited clearly the fundamental elements of the classic church orders. After a period of decline from that standard, the next milestone was reached with the publication of the *Church Book* (1868) by the General Council. Building on that English-language work, the General Synod and the United Synod in the South joined with the General Council to produce the Common Service (1888), forming it on the principle of "the common consent of the pure Lutheran liturgies of the sixteenth century." Further joint efforts resulted in the *Common Service Book* (1917), the appearance of which coincided with the formation of The United Lutheran Church in America, the merger of the three church bodies.

Meanwhile Lutheran immigrants continued to arrive. They formed new groupings of congregations. Swedes formed The Augustana Evangelical Lutheran Church. German groups centered in Buffalo, Iowa, Ohio, and Texas combined to form the American Lutheran Church. The Lutheran Church—Missouri Synod and other churches of the Evangelical Lutheran Synodical Conference of North America represented other segments of the northern European heritage. The Evangelical Lutheran Church and the Lutheran Free Church exemplified the Norwegian tradition. The American Evangelical Lutheran Church and the United Evangelical Lutheran Church were groupings of Danish congregations. The Finnish Evangelical-Lutheran Church of America (The Suomi Synod) completed the Scandinavian circle. As these churches began to worship in English, most of them eventually included the Common Service in their hymnals. The liturgical tradition was becoming uniform, but the hymn traditions remained diverse.

Eight churches began work in 1945 on a service book and hymnal through the Joint Commission on the Liturgy and Hymnal. The endeavor grew out of their desire for a common worship in a common tongue as a sign of a common Lutheran heritage. The desire to express more clearly the breadth of the ecumenical heritage in worship, part of the Lutheran birthright, also motivated their work. The step could be contemplated because of increased knowledge of liturgical origins and development, and also because of the dawning of a keener ecumenical awareness.

The *Service Book and Hymnal* (1958) was published jointly by the churches soon to form The American Lutheran Church (1960) and the Lutheran Church in America (1962). Liturgically, it marked both the culmination of the Common Service tradition and the first step into the larger ecumenical heritage. Musically, the liturgies continued the style of the *Common Service Book*, but added the northern European type of unison chant derived from plainsong and the chorale. The hymnal was conceived as a collection for Lutherans who had become Americans in speech and culture. It combined translations of Lutheran hymns from Germany and Scandinavia with English versions of Greek and Latin hymns, while giving preeminence to the Anglo-American tradition.

The Lutheran Church—Missouri Synod together with other churches of the Synodical Conference had published *The Lutheran Hymnal* in 1941 and was understandably reluctant to join a new project in 1945. The liturgy of *The Lutheran Hymnal* is similar to that in the *Common Service Book*, though with different musical settings in the style of Anglican chant. The hymns are predominantly Germanic in origin, preserving in translation not only the classic body of chorales but also many pietistic hymns of the eighteenth and nineteenth centuries.

At the beginning of the 1960s, most Lutherans in North America used either the *Service Book and Hymnal* or *The Lutheran Hymnal*. The liturgical traditions were similar in form and musical style; the hymnals were markedly different.

In 1965, after abandoning work on a project of its own begun in 1953, The Lutheran Church—Missouri Synod issued an invitation to other Lutheran churches in North America to join it in work toward a common hymnal and service book.[2] Groundwork for such a venture had been laid in joint work on *Culto Christiano* (1964), a book for Spanish-speaking Lutherans. The invitation was accepted by the Lutheran Church in America, the Synod of Evangelical Lutheran Churches (Slovak), and The American Lutheran Church, and in 1966 the Inter-Lutheran Commission on Worship was formed. Soon thereafter the Slovak church merged with The Lutheran Church—Missouri Synod, and was replaced as a partner in the ILCW by The Evangelical Lutheran Church of Canada, formerly the Canadian district of The American Lutheran Church.

The Inter-Lutheran Commission on Worship entered into dialog with congregations, pastor, musicians, and theologians on the basis of a series of trial-use booklets, *Contemporary Worship*.[3] These were supplemented with testing programs, conferences, and questionnaires. Congregations for whom the revised services and hymns are intended have been able to participate in shaping the project. The result is this *Lutheran Book of Worship*.[4]

An examination of the contents will reveal the several goals toward which the Commission worked in liturgy: to restore to Holy Baptism the liturgical rank and dignity implied by Lutheran theology, and to draw out the baptismal motifs in such acts as the confession of sin and the burial of the dead; to continue to move into the larger ecumenical heritage of liturgy, while at the same time enhancing Lutheran convictions about the Gospel; to involve lay persons as assisting ministers who share the leadership of corporate worship; to bring the language of prayer and praise into conformity with the best current usage; to offer a variety of musical styles.

Compilers of the hymnal have worked for an equitable balance among hymns of the various Lutheran language traditions, while acting on the premise that most North American Lutherans no longer regard themselves as transplanted Europeans. The Anglo-American hymn tradition is given, therefore, a rightful and large place. More early American tunes are included than in previous hymnals; fewer late nineteenth-century English tunes are included.

Through participation in groups such as the Consultation on Common Texts, the Consultation on Ecumenical Hymnody, and the International Consultation on English Texts, the Inter-Lutheran Commission on Worship has done its work in concert with other English-speaking churches. Through the Lutheran World Federation, contact has been maintained with other Lutheran churches of the world.

The services of the *Lutheran Book of Worship* embody the tradition of worship which received its characteristic shape during the early centuries of the Church's existence and was reaffirmed during the Reformation era. As such, they are an emblem of continuity with the whole Church and of particular unity with Lutherans throughout the world. At the same time, the services are adaptable to various circumstances and situations. Freedom and flexibility in worship is a Lutheran inheritance, and there is room for ample variety in ceremony, music, and liturgical form.

Having considered their resources and their customs, congregations will find their own balance between fully using the ritual and musical possibilities of the liturgy, and a more modest practice. A full service should not allow secondary ceremonies to eclipse central elements of the liturgy, nor should a simple service omit essential or important parts. Every service, whether elaborate or spare, sung or said, should be within the framework of the common rite of the Church, so that the integrity of the rite is always respected and maintained.

With informed and imaginative use, this book can open to congregations the riches of the Church's heritage of liturgy and song, and thus become a worthy instrument in the praise and thanksgiving of the people of God.

Notes

[1]*Lutheran Book of Worship* contains 569 hymns, three different musical settings for Holy Communion together with a Chorale setting for Holy Communion, Morning and Evening Prayer, Prayer at the Close of Day, The Litany, orders for Holy Baptism, Affirmation of Baptism, Marriage, Burial of the Dead, a large portion of the Psalter, plus several other services and indices. It also included—for the first time in an official American Lutheran hymnbook—a listing of the Hymn of the Day (*de tempore* hymn) for the church year.

[2]The story of the development of this joint project leading to *Lutheran Book of Worship* is told in "Convergence and Cooperation," Philip Pfatteicher, *Commentary on the Lutheran Book of Worship*. Minneapolis: Augsburg Fortress, 1990, pp. 1–12.

[3]These included the following booklets: *Contemporary Worship* (CW) 1: *Hymns* (1969); CW 2: *The Holy Communion* (1970); CW 3: *The Marriage Service* (1972); CW 4: *Hymns for Baptism and Holy Communion* (1972); CW 5: *Services of the Word* (1972); CW 6: *The Church Year: Calendar and Lectionary* (1973); CW 7: *Holy Baptism* (1974); CW 8: *Affirmation of the Baptismal Covenant* (1975); CW 9: *Daily Prayer of the Church* (1976); CW 10: *Burial of the Dead* (1976). In addition, a booklet titled *Contemporary Worship 01: The Great Thanksgiving* (1975) was also sent to all pastors of the cooperating churches.

[4]Members of the Inter-Lutheran Commission on Worship as well as the members of the various standing committees which produced the *Lutheran Book of Worship* are given in the acknowledgments on p. 922–923. Project Director for the ILCW was Eugene L. Brand (1976–78); music editor for the book was Richard Hillert.

27

Lutheran Worship[1]

Prepared by The Commission on Worship
of The Lutheran Church—Missouri Synod

Concordia Publishing House, St. Louis, Missouri, 1982

Our Lord speaks and we listen. His Word bestows what it says. Faith that is born from what is heard acknowledges the gifts received with eager thankfulness and praise. Music is drawn into this thankfulness and praise, enlarging and elevating the adoration of our gracious giver God.

Saying back to him what he has said to us, we repeat what is most sure and true. Most true and sure is his name, which he put upon us with the water of our Baptism. We are his. This we acknowledge at the beginning of the Divine Service. Where his name is, there is he. Before him we acknowledge that we are sinners, and we plead for forgiveness. His forgiveness is given us, and we, freed and forgiven, acclaim him as our great and gracious God as we apply to ourselves the words he has used to make himself known to us.

The rhythm of our worship is from him to us, and then from us back to him. He gives his gifts, and together we receive and extol them. We build one another up as we speak to one another in psalms, hymns, and spiritual songs. Our Lord gives us his body to eat and his blood to drink. Finally his blessing moves us out into our calling, where his gifts have their fruition. How best to do this we learn from his Word and from the way his Word has prompted his worship through the centuries. We are heirs of an astonishingly rich tradition. Each generation receives from those who went before and, in making that tradition of the Divine Service its own, adds what best may serve in its own day—the living heritage and something new.

Lutheran Worship, within its compass, seeks to carry forward the great heritage and add something new. The Common Service (Divine Service I), familiar to all Lutherans, is carried forward with no great changes and with some improvements where these seem needed. This will serve the continuity of our worship with an order of long-proven worth. In addition there is a service in two settings that derives from the work of the Inter-Lutheran Commission on Worship (Divine Service II, First Setting, and Divine Service II, Second Setting). Divine Service III draws on our treasury of chorales and revives the historic *Liedmesse*, a typically Lutheran contribution to worship form in which chorales largely replace chant.

There is also continuity with our familiar Matins and Vespers. In some places a better musical setting has been provided. In addition there are the Morning Prayer, Evening Prayer, and Prayer at the Close of the Day from the work of the Inter-Lutheran Commission on Worship. There are further orders for various occasions, so that altogether Lutheran Worship provides orders of service with a faithfulness to the Lutheran tradition and understanding of worship in the widest range of orders of service for English-speaking Lutherans.

In its hymnody each age of the Church reflects what it returns to God for the great blessings it has received from him. Some of the Church's song is always derived from a previous era. The early Church developed its music from the psalmody of the synagog, to which it added the strophic hymns of Greek and Roman converts. When the liturgy became the sole property of the clergy, there arose a need for hymns in the language of the people. Thus there came into being the great body of Latin hymns introduced and promoted by Bishop Ambrose of Milan and his followers. In time these again became the property of the clergy and hierarchy. The Lutheran Reformation once more restored the Church's song to the people in their native tongue. From then on the Lutheran Church became known as the "singing Church." The song of this Church has weathered and withstood such influences as pietism, rationalism, modernism, and universalism in one form or another.

The hymns in *Lutheran Worship* draw on the vast treasury of Christian hymnody old and new, with words that speak God's law and Gospel and express our faith's response and with music that nourishes both memory and heart.

Directed by the 1979 convention of The Lutheran Church—Missouri Synod in St. Louis,[2] the Commission on Worship offers this book for the enlivening and strengthening of worship, with gratitude for all those who have served the worship of our Lord and with the prayer that it may be serviceable to him and his people for the saving Gospel's sake.

Notes

[1]This collection contains 520 hymns, Divine Service I (a revision of the Common Service from *The Lutheran Hymnal*), Divine Service II, First and Second Settings (two different musical settings essentially from *Lutheran Book of Worship*), Divine Service III (chorale mass), Matins and Vespers, Morning and Evening Prayer, Prayer at the Close of Day, Responsive Prayer 1 and 2, The Litany, Holy Baptism, Confirmation, Luther's Small Catechism, other devotional helps, and indices.

[2]The wording of the synodical resolution noted that the Special Hymnal Review Committee created in 1977 had recommended that "the *Lutheran Book of Worship* be adopted with revision." The official language of The Lutheran Church—Missouri Synod continued to use the concept that the Missouri Synod book (to be called *Lutheran Worship*) would in fact be a revision of *Lutheran Book of Worship*. See *Convention Proceedings*, 53rd Regular Convention, The Lutheran Church—Missouri Synod, St. Louis, Missouri, July 6–12, 1979, pp. 113–17.

28

Christian Worship
A Lutheran Hymnal[1]

The Wisconsin Evangelical Lutheran Synod, formerly a member of the Synodical Conference, which had been using The Lutheran Hymnal *since 1941, had declined to participate in the work leading to either* Lutheran Book of Worship *or* Lutheran Worship. *Instead they determined to prepare their own book which they published as* Christian Worship: A Lutheran Hymnal (1993). *By the end of the century three books were now serving American Lutherans:* Lutheran Book of Worship, Lutheran Worship, *and* Christian Worship: A Lutheran Hymnal.

Christian Worship
A Lutheran Hymnal

Authorized by the Wisconsin Evangelical Lutheran Synod

Northwestern Publishing House, Milwaukee, Wisconsin, 1993

Introduction

The story of *Christian Worship: A Lutheran Hymnal* actually began in 1953 when The Lutheran Church—Missouri Synod (LCMS) initiated work on a revision of *The Lutheran Hymnal* (1941), the hymnal shared by the synods constituting the Synodical Conference. In 1959 the Wisconsin Evangelical Lutheran Synod (WELS) accepted the invitation to share in the revision work. In 1965, however, the LCMS abandoned this project in favor of a new pan-Lutheran hymnal, leading to the publication of *Lutheran Book of Worship* (1978) and *Lutheran Worship* (1982). After studying various options, the WELS in its 1983 convention resolved: "That the synod now begin work on a new/revised hymnal of its own, one that under the blessings of God will be scripturally sound and edifying, welcomed and judged to be highly satisfactory by a majority of our members, in harmony with the character and heritage of our church body, and reflecting the larger perspective and mainstream worship of the Christian church."

In 1984 the Conference of Presidents called a full-time project director[2] and appointed working committees. The Liturgy Committee, Hymn Committee, and Commission on Worship formed the Joint Hymnal Committee.[3] Later in the project a full-time music editor was called.[4] The hymnal group worked steadily for seven years to finish the hymnal manuscript, followed by a year and a half of layout, design, and promotion.[5] In 1993, the completed hymnal was introduced along with *Christian Worship: Accompaniment for Liturgy and Psalms*[6] and *Christian Worship: Manual.*[7]

The phrase "new/revised" in the synodical resolutions was interpreted to mean a hymnal which *preserved* the Christian and Lutheran heritage of liturgy and hymns from *The Lutheran Hymnal* and at the same time *improved* and *expanded* it. Much of the familiar content of *The Lutheran Hymnal* has been preserved. The three historic liturgies, the Common Service, Matins, and Vespers are retained with some revision. Two new liturgies are included, the Service of the Word and Sacrament and the Service of the Word, following the structure of historic Lutheran liturgy, but with new or revised texts and with newly composed music. These liturgies were added to provide some of the liturgical variety sought by many congregations and individuals. Also included in the book are rites for the Sacrament of Holy Baptism, Christian Marriage, and Christian Funeral. Three brief liturgies, Morning, Evening, and General Devotions, are designed for use in schools, conferences, and congregational organizations.

The regular use of Psalms is a new liturgical feature. In addition to its traditional use in Morning Praise and Evening Prayer (Matins and Vespers), the Psalm serves as response to the first lesson in the Common Service, Service of the Word and

Sacrament, and Service of the Word. The most important and most familiar of the Psalms were selected and arranged for liturgical use by carefully shortening to six or seven verses. All the psalms or psalm section are responsorial and have been furnished with easy and attractive congregational refrains. Sixteen melodies have been provided for singing psalm verses.

The hymn section of the new hymnal has a familiar look. Over 400 hymns have been retained from *The Lutheran Hymnal*, although many have undergone a slight updating of language. The hymns are arranged according to the Christian year and topical headings. The section also has a new look and sound. The last three decades have seen a strong resurgence of creativity and interest in the writing of hymns. Therefore, congregations will enjoy a greater variety of hymns than formerly. In addition to Lutheran chorales and traditional English hymnody, a wide selection of plainsong hymns, spirituals, folk hymns from Appalachia, Wales, Ireland, and elsewhere, gospel hymns, and contemporary hymns in different styles are included. In addition to new texts and new melodies, a somewhat freer and fresher type of harmonization has been furnished for some of the hymns; descants and guitar chords are supplied for a few others.

The hymnal is a unique tool for worship. It is a treasury of theology, poetry, music, history, liturgy, and praise. Because it is truly "the people's book," a good deal of care was taken to solicit opinion and reaction from the field. In addition to the *Sampler*[8] of liturgy, hymnody, psalmody, and prayer distributed to all congregations early in the project, field testing among groups of congregations was carried on throughout the project. Thanks is due the many critical reviewers, proofreaders, and writers of several thousand letters of advice and reaction.

The overall intent of those who prepared *Christian Worship: A Lutheran Hymnal* was to produce a Lutheran hymnal that was at once forward-looking and also enriched by the faith and worship experience of the whole Christian church of the past. Specifically the goal was to deliver to the church a strongly Christ-centered book, bringing together liturgies and a large number of hymns celebrating the life and atoning work of Jesus. May the new book continue to proclaim the power of the Word of God and the foundation doctrine of forgiveness by God's grace through faith in Christ. May its use among us foster and strengthen appreciation of liturgical worship and enrich and enliven our relationship with God and each other.[9]

IN THE NAME OF JESUS

Notes

[1]This volume contains 623 hymns, Holy Baptism, The Common Service adapted from *The Lutheran Hymnal*, a Service of Word and Sacrament, a Service of the Word, Morning Praise, Evening Prayer, 59 Psalm portions for singing, Christian Marriage, Christian Funeral, together with other devotional materials and indices.

[2]Rev Kurt J. Eggert.

[3]The Joint Hymnal Committee at the time of publication of *Christian Worship: A Lutheran Hymnal* consisted of C. T. Aufdemberge, Bruce Backer, Elfred Bloedel, Richard Buss, Theodore Hartwig, Mark Jeske, Iver Johnson, Harlyn Kuschel, Arnold Lehmann, Carl Nolte, Victor Prange, David Prillwitz, Loren Schaller, Wayne Schulz, and James Tiefel.

[4]Kermit G. Moldenhauer.

[5]The hymnal notes that special thanks in the development of the hymnal are due to the following: G. Jerome Albrecht (+), Martin Albrecht (+), David Bauer, Gary Baumler, Don Beutin, Mark Brunner, James Engel (+), James Fricke, Richard Hillert, Mentor Kujath, Laureen Reu Liu, Judith Lueck, Gordon Pape, Otto Schenk, Armin Schuetze, Sharon Uekert, David Vallesky, and Wayne and Esther Wiechmann. [+ deceased]

[6]*Christian Worship: Accompaniment for Liturgy and Psalms*. Authorized by the Wisconsin Evangelical Lutheran Synod. Milwaukee, Wisconsin: Northwestern Publishing House, 1993.

[7]*Christian Worship: Manual*. Gary Baumler & Kermit Moldenhauer, eds. Authorized by the Commission on Worship of the Wisconsin Evangelical Lutheran Synod. Milwaukee, Wisconsin: Northwestern Publishing House, 1993. The four sections of the manual are edited by James Tiefel, Wayne Schultz, Harlyn Kuschel, and Victor Prange. Contributors include Ames Anderson, Bruce Backer, Kris Altergott Eggers, Kurt Eggert, Bryan Gerlach, Theodore Hartwig, Harlyn Kuschel, Edward Meyer, Kermit Moldenhauer, Victor Prange, Wayne Schultz, George Tiefel, and James Tiefel.

[8]*Sampler. New Hymns and liturgy*. Milwaukee, Wisconsin: Northwestern Publishing House, 1986. This 60-page trial booklet contained 21 hymns, The Service, 12 Psalms with tones for chanting, and the Propers (Psalms and Verses). The Hymn Project personnel in 1986 consisted of the following: The Commission on Worship—Martin Albrecht, chairman; Gordon Pape, secretary; Clancy Aufdemberge; Bruce Backer; Elfred Bloedel; Theodore Hartwig; Victor Prange, Kurt Eggert, advisory. The Liturgy Committee—Victor Prange, chairman; Arnold Lehmann, secretary; Theodore Hartwig; Iver Johnson; Wayne Schulz; James Tiefel. The Hymn Committee—James Fricke, chairman; Mark Jeske, secretary; Bruce Backer; Richard Buss; Harlyn Kuschel; Kermit Moldenhauer. There were three representatives of the Evangelical Lutheran Synod: Erling Teigen, Walther Gullixson, and Paul Madson.

[9]Within the first year after its appearance, *Christian Worship: A Lutheran Hymnal* was being used by more than 90 percent of the more than 1200 parishes of the Wisconsin Evangelical Lutheran Synod.

Index

Carl Schalk, lecturer and clinician at numerous church music workshops and pastoral conferences, teaches graduate and undergraduate courses in church music as Distinguished Professor of Music at Concordia University, River Forest, and has been described as "one of the most active lecturers and clinicians on the American church music scene."

He holds advanced degrees from the Eastman School of Music, Rochester, New York (M. Mus.) and from Concordia Seminary, St. Louis, Missouri (M.A.R.). He has received honorary degrees from Concordia College, Seward, Nebraska (LL.D.) and Concordia College, St. Paul, Minnesota (LH.D.), and was named a Fellow of the Hymn Society of the United States and Canada.

He participated in the work leading to the publication of *Lutheran Book of Worship* (1978) and is a well–known composer of choral music, hymn settings for choir and congregation, and hymn tunes that appear in many current hymnals. He was the editor of *Church Music* journal (1966–80). He has served on numerous music boards and committees.

His most recent publications include *Luther on Music: Paradigms of Praise*; *The Praise of God in Song: An Introduction to Christian Hymnody for Congregational Study*; and *God's Song in a New Land: Lutheran Hymnals in America*.

Dr. Schalk is married to Noel Donata Roeder. They have three grown children.